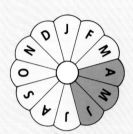

Poison Ivy and Poison Oak

This weed (above) causes an itchy rash if you touch it. Poison Ivy grows like a vine, and Poison Oak grows like a shrub. Try to remember what the leaves look like, and do not touch it. If you do touch it, washing your hands as soon as possible may reduce the itching. Your local drug store will have various remedies that will help.

Flowering Calendar

This flower symbol is shown alongside every plant. The red petals shows you at a glance in which months of the year the plant flowers. In the example shown here, the plant flowers from April to June.

SCIENCE NATURE GUIDES

WILD FLOWERS
OF NORTH AMERICA

Pam Forey

EDITED BY
Angela Royston

US CONSULTANT
Rick Imes

THUNDER BAY
P·R·E·S·S

Conservation

No flower grows in isolation from its surroundings. Each plant is part of a web of thousands of other plants and animals that live together. Different plants grow in different kinds of soil and climates. As you learn more about a habitat, you will get to know which flowers you could expect to find there.

Many habitats have been damaged or destroyed by pollution, agriculture, and industry. Some wild flowers are in danger of disappearing altogether because so many of their habitats have been disturbed or destroyed. On page 78, you will find the names of some organizations who campaign for the preservation of the countryside. By joining them and supporting their efforts, you can help to preserve our wild flowers and landscape.

As a general rule: don't pick flowers growing wild—you can study them just as easily where they are, and leave them to make seeds for next year's flowers. If you want to pick wild flowers, grow your own in a wilderness garden (see page 28). And, before you go walking in the country, make sure you read the Countryside Code below.

Countryside Code

1 **Ask permission before exploring** or crossing private property.
2 **Keep to footpaths** as much as possible.
3 **Leave fence gates as you find them.**
4 **Only pick a flower** growing wild if you are sure it is common.
5 **Only pick one or two flowers** and then only from a large clump.
6 **Leave the roots behind** of flowers you pick and don't dig up bulbs or plants to take home.
7 **Keep off crops** and don't walk on wild flowers.

Thunder Bay Press
5880 Oberlin Drive
Suite 400
San Diego, CA 92121

First published in the United States
by Thunder Bay Press, 1994

© Dragon's World 1994
Text © Dragon's World 1994
Illustrations © Dragon's World, 1994

Complete Cataloging in Publication (CIP) is available through the Library of Congress.
LC Card Number: 93-46146

Simplified text and captions by Angela Royston, based on *Wild Flowers of North America* by Pamela Forey.

Species illustrations by Norman Barber, Angela Beard, Richard Bell, Alma Hathaway, Roger Kent, David More, Susanna Stuart-Smith and David Thelwell, all of Bernard Thornton Artists, London.
Habitat paintings and headbands by Antonia Phillips.
Identification and activities illustrations by Richard Coombes.

Editor   Diana Briscoe
Designer   James Lawrence
Design Assistant Victoria Furbisher
Editorial Director Pippa Rubinstein

Printed in Spain

ISBN 1 85028 266 8

Contents

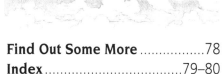

Introduction

There are thousands of different wild flowers in North America. Not only are they beautiful, but many are useful, too. You might be surprised at how many plants have been used as herbal medicines for hundreds of years.

Lots of wild plants used to be eaten raw or cooked, but others are extremely poisonous. You should never eat anything—flowers, leaves, seeds, or fruits—that you find growing wild. The chance of making a mistake is too great.

Being able to identify wild flowers is useful as well as fun. But, with so many different flowers that you might find, where do you start?

This book has been planned to help you in two ways. It shows only the flowers you are most likely to see and it groups them according to the habitat, or type of countryside, where you are most likely to see them. There are six main habitats described in this book, ranging from roadsides and city parks to desert.

The life of a plant

Look for plants at all stages of their life cycle, as buds and fruits as well as flowers. Dandelions are annuals—they die after producing seeds. To find out more about how plants reproduce and about pollination, see pages 18–19.

Biennials live for two growing seasons and perennials live for several years. Many perennials grow from a bulb (see page 28) or rhizome, which gives them a store of food to last them through the winter.

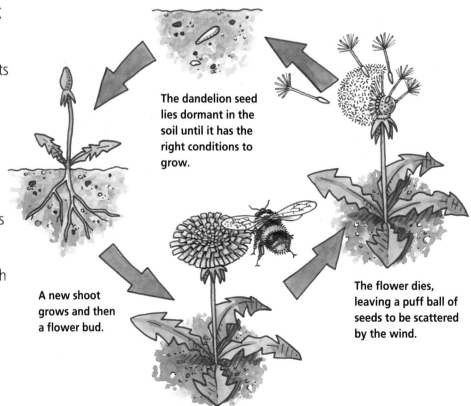

The dandelion seed lies dormant in the soil until it has the right conditions to grow.

The flower dies, leaving a puff ball of seeds to be scattered by the wind.

A new shoot grows and then a flower bud.

When the flower opens, insects move the pollen from the stamens to the stigma of the flower and the seeds are fertilized.

How to use this book

To identify a flower you do not recognize—for example, the climbing pink and the yellow flowers shown here—follow these steps.

1 **Decide what type of habitat you are in.** If you aren't sure, read the descriptions at the start of each section.

2 **What color is your flower?** Look through the pages of flowers with this color and heading. The picture and information given for each flower will help you identify it. The pink flower is Field Bindweed (on page 67).

3 **If you can't find the flower,** look for it under another color. Some flowers vary in color. White clover, for example, can have white or pink flowers.

4 **If you can't find the flower in that section,** look through other habitats for flowers of that color. Some flowers grow in more than one kind of habitat. The white flower is Queen Anne's Lace (on page 65).

5 **If you still can't find the flower,** you may have to look in a larger field guide (see page 78 for suggestions). You may have found something that is very rare!

Top-of-page Picture Bands

Each habitat has a different picture band at the top of the page—they are shown below.

 Eastern Forests

Grasslands

Western Forests

 Wetlands

 Deserts

Roadsides & Parks

What To Look For

Parts of a flower

The shapes of flowers and the color of their petals may be very different from one kind of plant to another, but all flowers have the same parts and fulfill the same purpose. They make seeds so that the plant can reproduce itself. To do this the male pollen has to fertilize the female ovules.

Members of the daisy family, among others, have lots of tiny flowers packed into one composite flower head.

These strap-like petals are really tiny flowers called ray florets.

Each floret has its own ovary.

The centre of this daisy is made up of tiny flowers called disk florets.

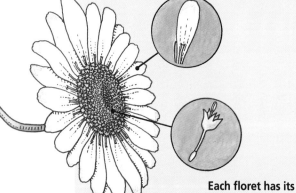

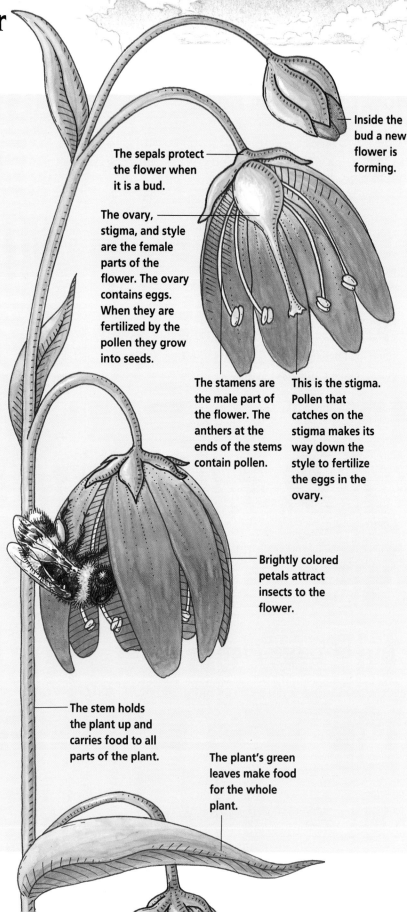

Inside the bud a new flower is forming.

The sepals protect the flower when it is a bud.

The ovary, stigma, and style are the female parts of the flower. The ovary contains eggs. When they are fertilized by the pollen they grow into seeds.

The stamens are the male part of the flower. The anthers at the ends of the stems contain pollen.

This is the stigma. Pollen that catches on the stigma makes its way down the style to fertilize the eggs in the ovary.

Brightly colored petals attract insects to the flower.

The stem holds the plant up and carries food to all parts of the plant.

The plant's green leaves make food for the whole plant.

Arrangement of flowers

Some plants have a single flower, others have clusters of flowers. Look for the particular shapes of clusters.

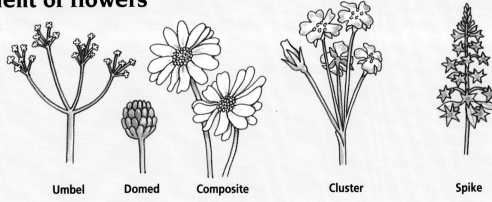

Umbel **Domed** **Composite** **Cluster** **Spike**

Shapes of leaves

Always check the shape of the leaves of a plant. They are sometimes the only way to tell one plant from another that is like it.

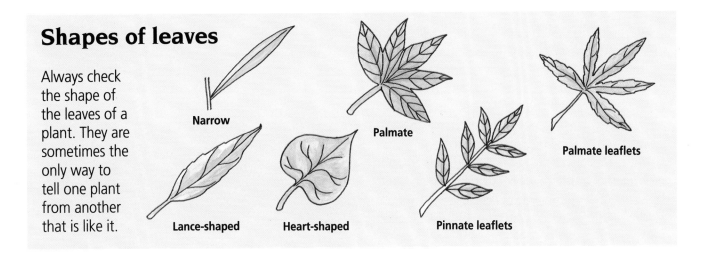

Narrow

Palmate

Palmate leaflets

Lance-shaped **Heart-shaped** **Pinnate leaflets**

How leaves grow

Leaves grow in different ways up the stem. Look for these arrangements.

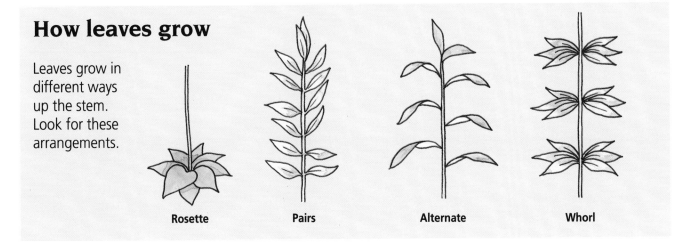

Rosette **Pairs** **Alternate** **Whorl**

Eastern Forests

There are several kinds of eastern forests, each with its own kinds of plants and flowers growing there. In the North are the great forests of spruce and fir. In the northeastern United States are areas of beech, maples, and birch. Farther south you will find oaks and hickories. The Appalachians have their own kind of forest and along the coast are the southern pine forests.

As you climb up a mountain, the forest changes in just the same way as if you were moving from south to north. All forests provide similar opportunities and problems for plants and flowers growing there. Trees need a lot of water, so forests grow only where there is plenty of rain. Rotting leaves keep the soil fertile and damp.

But plants also need sunlight and trees keep the ground cool and shady. Look for most woodland flowers in the spring. These flowers race to grow, flower, and fruit before the trees get their leaves and block out most of the sunshine. Most are perennials, growing year after year from bulbs, rhizomes, or tubers—swollen underground stems or roots that store enough food and energy to last the plant until the next spring.

In the late spring and summer you will still find flowers in the forest, but look for most of them where more sunlight filters through—along paths, in clearings, and on the edge of the forest. The picture shows eight flowers from this book. How many can you recognize?

Wild Columbine, Goatsbeard, Trumpet Honeysuckle, Indian Pipe, Jack-in-the-pulpit, Smooth Solomon's Seal, Starflower, Purple Trillium.

Eastern Forests

May Apple

Don't touch May Apple. It's poisonous and can irritate your skin. You are most likely to see it as a carpet of leaves covering the ground. Each stem has one or two large, umbrella-like leaves which have deep lobes. The flowers grow only on stems with two leaves. They are white and waxy and large yellow berries appear after the flowers die.

Barberry family
12–18 ins tall
Flowers in April-June
Also grows on shady roadsides

Wild Sarsaparilla

The round, greenish white flowers of Wild Sarsaparilla grow in a ball-shaped cluster at the end of a long flower stalk. The leaves grow on long stalks, too. They have three sections, each divided into leaflets. The fruits are dark blue-black berries. Wild Sarsaparilla grows from an underground stem, or rhizome, which the Indian tribes brewed to make tea or root beer, or made into a stimulating medicine.

Ginseng family
6–15 ins tall
Flowers in May-June

Wintergreen

These small, white flowers look like bells drooping from the base of the leaves. Look for this plant in the winter, too. As its name tells you, the leaves are evergreen, and the berries, which ripen in the late summer, often stay on the plant all winter. Oil of Wintergreen is used to flavor cough drops, toothpaste, and even candy. The plant is sometimes called Checkerberry or Teaberry.

Heath family
Creeping stem with branches 2–6 ins tall
Flowers in April-May
Also grows on mountainsides

Starflower

Look for these delicate star-like flowers in the cool, peaty woods of Canada and the northern US. Each stem has two flowers, which grow on short stalks from the center of a whorl of five or six, dark green, shiny leaves. The petals have golden-yellow anthers.

Primrose family
4–8 ins tall
Flowers in May-June

Nodding Trillium

The single white flower of NoddingTrillium hangs, or nods, underneath the leaves. The flower has three white petals and a long stalk. The three oval, pointed leaves grow in a whorl near the top of the stem. Several similar white flowers grow in the East but their flowers don't hang like those of Nodding Trillium.

Lily family
6–18 ins tall – Flowers in March-June
Grows in damp woods

Partridgeberry

Look for this plant trailing on the ground. The tubular flowers are white or pink, and grow in pairs. See how they are joined at the base and grow from the base of the uppermost leaves. The shiny leaves are evergreen, and grow in pairs along the branching stems. The flowers are followed by red berries, which remain on the plant into the winter.

Bedstraw (or Madder) family
Creeping stem
Flowers in May-June
Sometimes grown in gardens

Bloodroot

These white flowers grow from a stout underground stem, called a rhizome. The single leaves are blue-green, round, and have lobes. The rhizomes have a burning red sap. The plant has been used as a herbal medicine to treat skin problems like eczema and ringworm, but less painful remedies are used now.

Poppy family
About 10 ins tall
Flowers in March-April
Also grown in gardens

Eastern Forests

Smooth Solomon's Seal

Look for Solomon's Seal growing in the shade. The greenish white flowers are shaped like bells. See how they grow in ones or twos along the arching stem at the base of each pair of leaves. The leaves are broad and oval. After the flowers die the stems are hung with blue-black berries.

Lily family
Up to 3 ft tall – Flowers in May-June

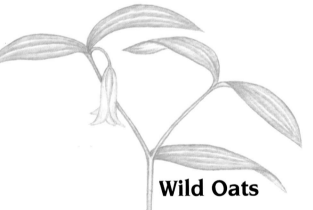

Wild Oats

Lily family
Up to 1 ft tall
Flowers in April-June
Also grows in mountains in the South

The drooping creamy-yellow flowers of this delicate-looking plant are shaped like long, narrow bells and grow at the end of the stem. See how the stem grows straight and leafless out of the ground. Then it forks near the top into two leafy branches. The leaves are narrow and pointed. The stems grow from a slender, underground rhizome.

Red Baneberry

Be careful—Red Baneberry is very poisonous if eaten! Its white flowers grow in thick clusters at the end of a long flowering stalk. The petals soon fall, leaving behind many white stamens. Look at the leaves. They are very large and divided into several toothed leaflets, each about 2–3 inches long. The flowers are followed by clusters of poisonous red berries.

Buttercup or Crowfoot family
12–24 ins tall
Flowers in May-July

Downy Yellow Violet

There are several kinds of yellow violet, and each has five yellow petals. You can tell this is the Downy Yellow Violet because it is covered with soft hairs. Look carefully at the flowers. They should have purple-brown veins on the lower petal. The leaves are 2–5 inches wide. They are heart-shaped with large, rounded teeth.

Violet family
Up to 16 ins tall
Flowers in March-April
Grows in damp or shady places

Bluebead Lily

Bluebead Lily is also known as the Corn Lily. It has a cluster of three to eight, greenish yellow flowers. They are shaped like bells and grow at the end of a long flowering stalk. They are followed by bluish berries. The glossy green leaves are oval and pointed. See how they curl at the base around the stem. Each plant has two to five leaves which grow from a knotty underground rhizome.

Lily family
Up to 15 ins tall – Flowers in May-August
Also grows on southern mountainsides

Dutchman's Breeches

This plant gets its name from its flowers. Breeches are short pants tied under the knee and these flowers look like white breeches hanging upside down from the flower stalks. Look at the clumps of leaves, too. They are gray-green and feathery. They grow in clumps each year from swollen underground roots, called tubers.

Fumitory family
About 6–12 ins tall
Flowers in March-April
Also grown in gardens

Goatsbeard

You will easily see this tall plant. It gets its name from its plumes of white, fluffy flowers. Look at the leaves, too. They are up to 15 inches long and divided into leaflets. Each leaflet is oblong and pointed, and has a jagged edge.

Rose family
Up to 6 ft tall
Flowers in May-July
Also grown in gardens

Yellow Lady's-slipper

Lady's-slippers are sometimes called Moccasin Flowers. Both names come from the shape of the flower, whose pouched lips look like a slipper. Look for the magenta spots inside the pouched, yellow lips. Look at the yellow to purple wavy sepals, too. One points up and the other two point down. See how the ribbed, oval leaves grab the stem.

Orchid family
Up to 2 ft tall – Flowers in May-June
Also grows in swamps and other parts of North America

Jack-in-the-pulpit

This tall plant has only one or two large leaves divided into three leaflets. You may not see the flower at first. It grows under the leaves and has an arching leafy hood. The hood is green with maroon to whitish streaks. Look under the hood to see the green to brown, club-like spike, called a spathe, covered with tiny flowers. They are followed by a cluster of orange berries later in the season.

Arum family
1–3 ft tall
Flowers in March-April
Grows in wet woodlands

Indian Pipe

You can't mistake this strange-looking plant. Look for it in leaf trash in damp woodlands in the summer. It grows in clumps of white fleshy stems. They each bend over at the top into a white bell-like flower. The leaves are translucent and look like scales on the stem.

Indian Pipe family
Up to 9 ins tall
Flowers in June-August
Also found in damp woods all over North America

Clammy Ground Cherry

This plant is sticky rather than clammy. The heart-shaped, toothed leaves are covered with sticky hairs. Look for the bell-shaped flowers which hang from the base of the leaf stalks. They are greenish yellow with purple centers. They are followed by papery sacs which enclose the fruit—yellow tomato-like berries.

Nightshade family
Up to 3 ft tall – Flowers in June-September
Also grows in grasslands

Spring Beauty

Spring Beauty is a delicate plant with a sweet smell. Its white or pink flowers are striped with darker pink and grow in a cluster at the top of the stem. Each one has only two leaves. They are long and narrow, and grow opposite each other halfway up. Several stems grow from one fleshy corm hidden underneath the ground.

Purslane family – Up to 1 ft tall
Flowers in the spring and early summer
Also found in fields and clearings

Nodding Wild Onion

You can identify this plant by its leaves, which smell like onions when crushed. The nodding clusters of pink flowers appear around the middle of the summer, but the clumps of long, soft, narrow leaves start to grow in the early summer. Nodding Wild Onion belongs to the same family as wild leeks and garlics, and is one of the best for eating. The bulbs from which it grows are like cultivated onions and the leaves are good in salads.

Lily family
Up to 2 ft tall
Flowers in June-August
Also found in grasslands

Round-lobed Hepatica

The flowers may be white, pink, or lavender-blue. Although they look like regular flowers, they have no petals, but six petal-like sepals instead. This Hepatica is named for its leaves, which are divided into three rounded lobes. People used to think the leaves looked like the shape of the human liver. Hepaticas are sometimes called Liverleafs or Liverworts, and were used unsuccessfully to treat liver diseases.

Buttercup family
4–6 ins tall
Flowers in March-April

Eastern Forests

Wood Lily

Wood Lily has reddish orange flowers with dark spots which point up. The three petals and three petal-like sepals have narrow bases. There are six long, reddish orange stamens with large anthers. Its leaves are lance-shaped and grow in whorls of 3–8 leaves.

Lily family
1–3 ft tall
Flowers in June-August
Grows in dry woodlands

Wood Betony

You can recognize this flower from the thick clusters of red, yellow, or red or yellow flowers that grow at the top of the stems. Each flower has two lips. Look at the finely-cut leaves, too. Wood Betony, like other Louseworts, is partly a parasite. Their roots attach themselves to the roots of other plants and steal their water and nutrients.

Snapdragon or Figwort family
6–18 ins tall
Flowers in April-June
Also grows in grasslands

Bee Balm

These tall, bright red flower heads are hard to miss. Look for the reddish bracts under the flowers. Look at the flowers, too. Each has a longish tube and two lips. If you are lucky you might see a hummingbird eating the nectar. The leaves are lance-shaped and toothed, and grow in pairs up the long stems. Oil of bergamot is produced from the plant and is used to flavor tea.

Mint family
Up to 5 ft tall
Flowers in June-August
Also grows on mountainsides and in gardens

Purple Trillium

This deep red or maroon flower has three petals and three green sepals, which you can see in between the petals. It smells like rotting meat, but that attracts the flies which pollinate it. Its whorl of three diamond-shaped leaves grow at the top of the stem, underneath the flower.

Lily family
8–16 ins tall
Flowers in April-June

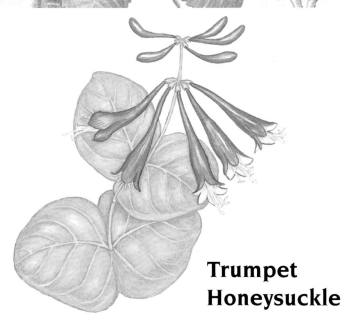

Trumpet Honeysuckle

This Honeysuckle is a climbing plant whose stems twine into the branches of shrubs and trees. You will easily see the whorls of brilliantly colored, trumpet-shaped flowers. They are red on the outside and yellow inside. They are rich in nectar and attract many insects and hummingbirds. Look at the pairs of oval leaves, too. Those underneath the flowers join across the stem to form a disk.

Honeysuckle family
Climbing vine – Flowers in April-August

Fire Pink

These crimson flowers often form large patches of color in open woods and rocky places. They grow in clusters at the ends of the weak stems. Look closely at one of the flowers. It has five narrow petals which grow from a long tube of sticky sepals. The leaves are long and narrow and grow in twos or fours.

Pink family
6–24 ins tall
Flowers in April-June

Garden Phlox

You will easily spot these showy, pink flowers. They grow in clusters at the end of a tall, leafy stem. The flowers are followed by capsules of seeds. The plant then dies, but grows up again the next year.

Phlox family
Up to 6 ft tall
Flowers in August-October
Also grown in gardens

Wild Columbine

These flowers are easy to recognize. The nodding red and yellow flowers are formed from red sepals and red and yellow petals. The nectar is inside the hollow "claws" of the petals. The delicate leaves are divided into groups of three leaflets.

Buttercup or Crowfoot family
2-4 ft tall – Flowers in April-July
Also grows in rocky places

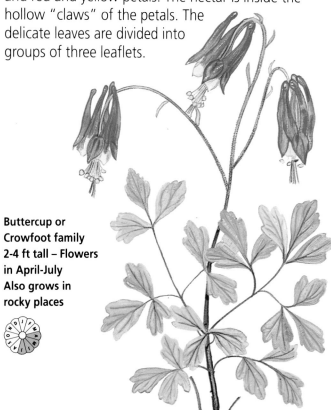

How Plants Make Seeds

Plants produce eggs (known as ovules) in the female part of the flower (the ovary), and pollen grains in the male part of the flower (the anthers). If you don't know where these parts of the flower are, look at pages 6 and 7, which tell you "what to look for." Pollen grains are carried from one flower to another by the wind, or by animals, usually insects.

Stigma — Pollen

Anthers

Style

Ovary
Ovules

Insects are attracted to flowers by their bright petals, their scent, and their sweet-tasting nectar. As they feed on the nectar and pollen, some pollen sticks to their bodies and is rubbed off on the next flower they visit.

If it is pollen from the same kind of flower and it sticks to the stigma, the pollen grows a tube to travel down the style into the ovary. There each grain of pollen joins with one ovule to fertilize it and produce a seed.

When most of the ovules have been fertilized by a pollen grain, the petals begin to wither and die. The seeds swell and grow in the ovary until they are ready to be scattered.

Pollinating a tomato plant

Only the right sort of pollen will fertilize the ovules. In this experiment you are the pollinator. You will take the pollen from one flower to another.

1 **Buy one or two tomato plants** and plant them in pots of compost. Use large pots, because the plants will grow up to 5 feet tall. Put them in a sunny place and water them regularly.

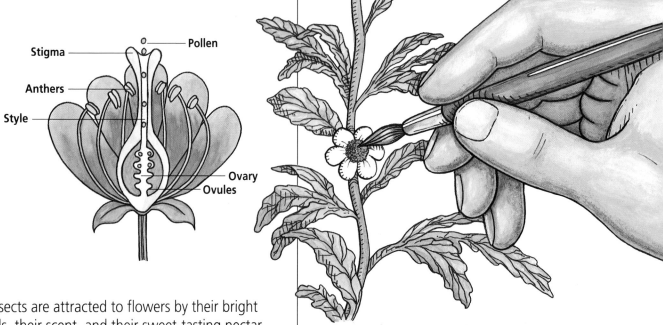

2 **When the flowers open**, you can use an artist's paint brush to transfer pollen from one flower to another. Push the brush into the flower and gently wiggle it about. Then push the brush into another flower and do the same thing.

3 **To test whether the pollen from another flower will fertilize the ovules**, first collect pollen from a different kind of flower—a geranium or poppy for example—and pollinate one flower on the tomato plant. Tie a bit of thread loosely around its stalk so that you can remember which flower you used for this test.

4 **Now pollinate the other tomato flowers** with tomato pollen. Use a clean paint brush every time you use a different sort of pollen.

5 **Carefully place a large, clear plastic bag over the plant** when you have finished pollinating, and tie it around the pot. This stops other pollens reaching the flowers.

6 **As soon as the flowers wither,** you can take the plastic bag off.

7 **Which flowers develop into tomatoes?** The flowers with the thread around the stalk, which you pollinated with geranium pollen, should not. If they do, it is because they were already pollinated with tomato pollen beforehand.

Scattering seeds

Flowers use many different methods to spread their seeds as widely as possible. Dandelions produce many seeds, each with a "parachute," which is blown in the wind. Only a few will land where they can grow, but that is enough to ensure survival.

Some seeds have tiny hooks which cling to your clothes or to the fur of animals.

Many seeds are wrapped in tasty berries which are snapped up by birds and other animals. The berries are eaten, but the seeds are dropped, or they may pass right through the animal's body and start to grow miles away from the parent flower.

Lupines, vetches, and other members of the pea and bean family have pods of seeds that burst open when they are ripe and scatter their seeds in all directions.

Poppy heads explode to scatter their seeds.

Seeds with burrs stick to clothes or fur.

Dandelion seeds have their own "parachutes."

Berries are eaten by birds and animals, and carried away by them.

Waterlily seeds float away from their parent plant.

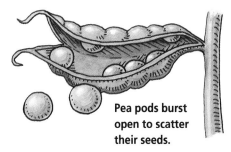

Pea pods burst open to scatter their seeds.

Grasslands

Grasslands get less rain than forests but more rain than deserts. Here you will find miles of land covered with grasses and wild flowers. The flowers that grow here like full sunshine, so look for them in the late spring, summer, and fall.

Water is scarce on the grasslands. Much of the rain evaporates in the wind and sun. Wild flowers that grow here have found their own ways of getting and conserving wate, like the large taproots that reach deep into the soil for water. Some are covered with dense white or silvery hairs. The hairs reflect some of the sun's rays and protect the plant from the drying wind.

The prairies are the largest grasslands in North America, but there are other areas of grassland in the Southwest, California, and between the Rocky Mountains and the more western mountains of the Sierra Nevada and the Cascade Range.

The prairies change from shortgrass in the West, where there is less rain, to tall grass in the East where more rain falls. Much of the tall grass prairie has been taken over for agriculture or by forest and only isolated areas remain, along railroads, for example. The picture shows seven flowers from this book. How many can you recognize?

Golden Aster, Tahaka Daisy, Wild Flax, Scarlet Globemallow, Sego Lily, Pasque Flower, Western Wallflower.

Blue Yucca

You can't miss this tall flowering stem with its many waxy bell-like flowers. The flowers are creamy-white on the inside, but often tinged with purple on the outside. The flower heads grow from a clump of sword-like spine-tipped leaves about 3 feet high. The flowers are followed by edible fleshy pods, which taste like sweet potatoes when they are baked.

Agave family
Up to 5 ft tall
Flowers in April-July
Also found in
deserts and scrub

Sego Lily

This white flower is the state flower of Utah. It grows in clusters at the top of the stem. Look at the complicated yellow and red markings around the center of the petals. Look for the beard inside the flower, too. The leaves are long and narrow, and often roll upward at the edges. Like other Mariposa Lilies, it grows from a bulb, that the Native Americans used to eat.

Lily family
Up to 18 ins tall – Flowers in May-July
Also grows in woods and sagebrush

Prairie Star

This plant is also called Starflower because of its small, star-like flowers. Look closely at the white or pinkish petals. They are divided into three or five lobes. The flowers open just as the clumps of leaves at the base are emerging and growing larger. The leaves are lobed and are hairy, too.

Saxifrage family
Up to 20 ins tall – Flowers in March-April
Also grows in dry woods, in sagebrush, and on the lower slopes of the Rocky Mountains

Canada Anemone

These white flowers grow at the end of a long stem. They don't have petals, but the five sepals look like petals. The leaves, like buttercup leaves, are palmate. Those at the base have long stalks, but look at those on the stem. They have no stalks at all, and are a sure way of identifying the plant. The flowering stems and leaves both grow from long, underground stems.

Buttercup or Crowfoot family
1–2 ft tall – Flowers in May-July
Also grows in meadows and thickets

Golden Aster

The yellow flower heads of Golden Aster grow in clusters at the ends of the stems. The center of each is yellow and, as the flower gets older, the surrounding, yellow ray florets begin to roll underneath. Before the flowers appear, you may see the plant as mounds of gray, branched, leafy stems. The gray color comes from the small, lance-shaped leaves that are thickly covered with hairs.

Sunflower or Daisy family
Up to 20 ins tall
Flowers in May-October
Also found on roadsides and hillsides

Common Sunflower

You can't miss these large yellow flower heads. Many measure 6 inches across. They are purplish brown in the center surrounded by bright yellow ray florets. They grow on tall, branching, leafy stems. Look for the oval or triangular leaves. They are toothed and rough and grow up to 1 foot long. The seeds can be eaten like the ones from cultivated sunflowers.

Sunflower or Daisy family
Up to 10 ft tall – Flowers in July-September

Little Golden Zinnia

This bright yellow-orange flower is also called the Plains Zinnia. It has a reddish central disk and only three to six, round, yellow ray florets surrounding it. It grows in low clumps and you may not see it until late summer when it is suddenly covered with flower heads. The linear leaves grow in pairs up the branching stems.

Sunflower or Daisy family
3–9 ins tall – Flowers in June-August
Also grows in deserts

Plains Prickly Pear

You will easily recognize prickly pears with their long flattened stems made up of oval sections 2–6 inches long. The flowers are yellow or red, and are followed by prickly fruits. Wear thick gloves if you pick them. The flowers and stems have many fine bristles in between the tufts of long spines. These gray, woolly bristles will irritate your skin more than the spikes.

Cactus family
4–24 ins tall – Flowers in May-June

Western Wallflower

Wallflowers are often seen growing in gardens, but the Western Wallflower is a spectacular wild variety. The flowers may be yellow, burnt-orange, or brick-red. They yield to slender, rectangular pods, that grow straight up at first, then slope out from the stem. The leaves are lance-shaped and alternate up the stem.

Mustard family
Up to 3 ft tall
Flowers in March-July

Indian Blanket

You can't miss this bright, showy flower. It is also called Showy Gaillardia, or sometimes Firewheel because its outer red petals have yellow ends. Look for the three deep teeth in each ray. Each flower head grows at the end of its own branch of the long stem. See how bristly the lobed leaves are.

Sunflower or Daisy family
12–24 ins tall – Flowers in May-July
Also grows on roadsides and in gardens

Cream Cups

These flowers vary in color from creamy-white to yellow, or white with yellow spots on the base of the petals. Like other poppies, they have many stamens in the center of the flower. Each plant has several hairy stems. The soft, hairy, linear leaves grow opposite each other on the lower half of the stem. Look for the fruit. The ovary separates into many sections that grow upward when the fruit forms.

Poppy family
4–12 ins tall
Flowers in March-May

Grasslands

Prairie Smoke

You are most likely to see this flower when it has gone to seed and looks like a feather duster. The flowers are reddish brown or pink, nodding, and urn-shaped. They yield to seeds with long, feathery hairs. The plant is hairy and has clumps of pinnate leaves at its base. Notice how the small leaflets alternate with larger ones.

Rose family
6–16 ins tall – Flowers in April-July
Also grows in woods

Indian Paintbrush

The flowers are greenish yellow, but are hardly seen at the base of the bright orange and scarlet, fan-shaped bracts. They get their name from an Native American legend about a brave who became frustrated while trying to paint a prairie sunset—the Great Spirit made these flowers spring up where he threw down his brushes. The leaves alternate up the stem and are divided into several narrow lobes.

Snapdragon or Figwort family
12–24 ins tall – Flowers in May-July

Sagebrush Mariposa Tulip

Look for this unusual-shaped flower in much the same places as Sego Lily (see page 21) to which it is closely related. The three, broad, pink or lilac petals are marked with yellow hairs and a crescent of dark red. See the three narrow sepals between the petals which are longer than them. There are several narrow, grass-like leaves on the stem.

Lily family – 6–24 ins tall
Flowers in May-August
Also grows in woods
and sagebrush

Queen of the Prairie

You can't miss these large, fluffy, pink clumps. Look closely to see how they are made up of sprays of tiny, sweet-scented flowers. Look at the dark green leaves, too. They are pinnate with many toothed leaflets. This flower is less common in the East and South, where any you see have probably escaped from yards.

Rose family
Up to 6 ft tall
Flowers in
June-August
Also grown in
gardens

Showy Evening Primrose

As its name tells you, this flower opens only in the evening. During the day you will only see the white or pink, nodding buds. The flowers grow from the base of the leaves that are lance-shaped and have shallow lobes. You might also see this plant east of the prairies, growing in waste places and on roadsides.

Evening Primrose family
Up to 2 ft tall – Flowers in May-July
Also grown in gardens

Rough Blazing Star

You can't miss these long spikes of bright purple, fluffy flower heads. Unusually, the flower heads open from the top of the spike downward. Each one grows from the base of a leaf. The leaves are narrow and grow in a clump at the base of the stem, and then alternate up the stem. Blazing Stars are also called Gayfeathers, because of their fluffy appearance.

Sunflower or Daisy family
1–4 ft tall
Flowers in August-October
Also found in open woods

Scarlet Globemallow

These brick-red or reddish orange flowers grow in spikes at the end of the weak stems, which are covered with soft, velvety hairs. Those at the bottom of the spike open first. Look for the fruits. They grow in a circle and are also covered with hairs. The leaves are rounded and have deep lobes. The stems grow from a woody taproot.

Mallow family
Up to 20 ins tall
Flowers in April-August
Also grows on roadsides

Grasslands

Tahaka Daisy

This plant has lots of flower heads, each with a yellow central disk surrounded by blue-purple petals. To be sure that it is a Tahaka Daisy, check its leaves. They are divided and look like the leaves of Tansy (see page 71), so the plant is sometimes called Tansy Aster.

Sunflower or Daisy flower
4–6 ins tall
Flowers in May-September

Crazyweed

Look for the bright pink or lavender flower clusters standing up above the leaves. Look at the tufts of leaves, too. Each leaf has 11 to 17 narrow leaflets covered with silvery, silky hairs. The flowers are followed by plump, oblong, pointed seed pods, that stand up. Like many other Locoweeds, this plant is well known to be poisonous to sheep and cattle.

Pea and Bean family
Up to 15 ins tall – Flowers in April-July

Pasque Flower

This flower is the state flower of South Dakota. It is a small plant, and is thickly covered with hairs. The flowers are purple, lavender, or blue with yellow stamens. They grow from the end of a long stalk. They are followed by clumps of deeply cut leaves. As the flowers die and the fruits ripen, the seeds develop long, feathery tips.

Buttercup or Crowfoot family
Up to 15 ins tall
Flowers in May-August

Leadplant

You can't miss these thick, blue flower heads. Look closely at the flowers. They each have only one blue petal and ten bright orange stamens. The leaves are divided into 15 to 45 crowded leaflets. They are covered with white hairs, making them look gray. The flowers are followed by seed pods that are also hairy.

Pea and Bean family
Up to 3 ft tall
Flowers in May-August

Silver Scurf Pea

This plant looks silvery due to the silky white hairs that cover it. The tiny flowers are very dark blue, but their sepals have silver hairs. They grow in small clusters on long stalks rising from the upper leaves. The leaves are divided into three to five oval leaflets. The flowers are followed by silky pods that contain one seed each.

Pea and Bean family
Up to 2 ft talll
Flowers in June-August

Elegant Brodiaea

Look for these clusters of reddish purple or purple flowers growing on bare stalks that grow upward. Notice how the petals join to make a funnel-shaped flower. You won't see the grassy leaves because they have already withered before the flowers open. The leaves and flowering stems grow each year from a short underground stem called a corm.

Lily family
Up to 15 ins tall
Flowers in April-July
Grows in California and Oregon

Baby Blue Eyes

See how these pale blue flowers are almost white at the center. They can measure over 1 inch across and are shaped like bowls. They grow on thin stalks near the ends of the stems. Look for the compound leaves divided into pinnate, toothed leaflets, too. The stems are thin and branched. The flowers are followed by capsules of seeds.

Waterleaf family
6–12 ins tall
Flowers in March-April
Also found on hillsides, sage scrub, chaparral, and near the West Coast

Wild Flax

You can recognize this plant from its loose clusters of sky blue flowers and lots of tiny, erect leaves that alternate up its stems. Look closely at the flowers. Each has five petals and five sepals. Wild Flax is related to Common Flax which is grown commercially and made into linseed oil and linen.

Flax family
1–2ft tall
Flowers in May-July
Also grown in gardens

Growing Your Own

Instead of picking flowers from the wild, why not grow your own in pots, window boxes, or in your yard. Look for packets of wild-flower seeds in your local garden center. When they flower, you can pick as many as you like.

Creating a wilderness

Birds and insects love weeds and wild plants. Ask your parents if you can make a special corner of your yard into a wilderness. All you have to do is leave it to run wild. Let the grass grow and soon you will have dandelions, buttercups, clover, and other common flowers growing there too.

Whatever you do, don't weed it! Buy a packet of wild flower seeds and scatter them there as well. Leave any fallen leaves to rot. Put some old logs and big stones in there too.

Then sit back and watch. Pill bugs and other insects will soon move in on the old leaves and logs. Birds will come to feed on them. In the summer bumblebees, butterflies, and other insects will pollinate the flowers.

Keep a record of the flowers that grow and the animals that visit. If you can, make a small pond and grow water plants in it. You may soon find tadpoles and frogs in there too.

Grow flowers from bulbs

Many of the earliest spring flowers grow from bulbs. The bulb is a store of food that lets the plant shoot up and grow before it is warm enough for most flowers. **Only use bulbs that you can buy—never dig up bulbs that are growing wild.**

1 **Buy your bulbs in the fall** and plant them in pots of compost, or garden soil mixed with sand. Dampen the compost before you begin.
2 **Half fill the pot with soil or compost**, then plant the bulbs with the pointed end upward. Leave about 1 inch between them. Cover them with soil until only the tips show.
3 **Leave the bulbs in a dark, airy place** until they begin to grow. Don't forget about them and be sure to keep the compost damp.
4 **You should see the first shoots** in about two months. Put the pots in a warm, sunny place and water them.

Try planting pips from apples or oranges, and the pits from avocados or peaches as well. Plant them as above, put them on a window sill, and keep them well watered.

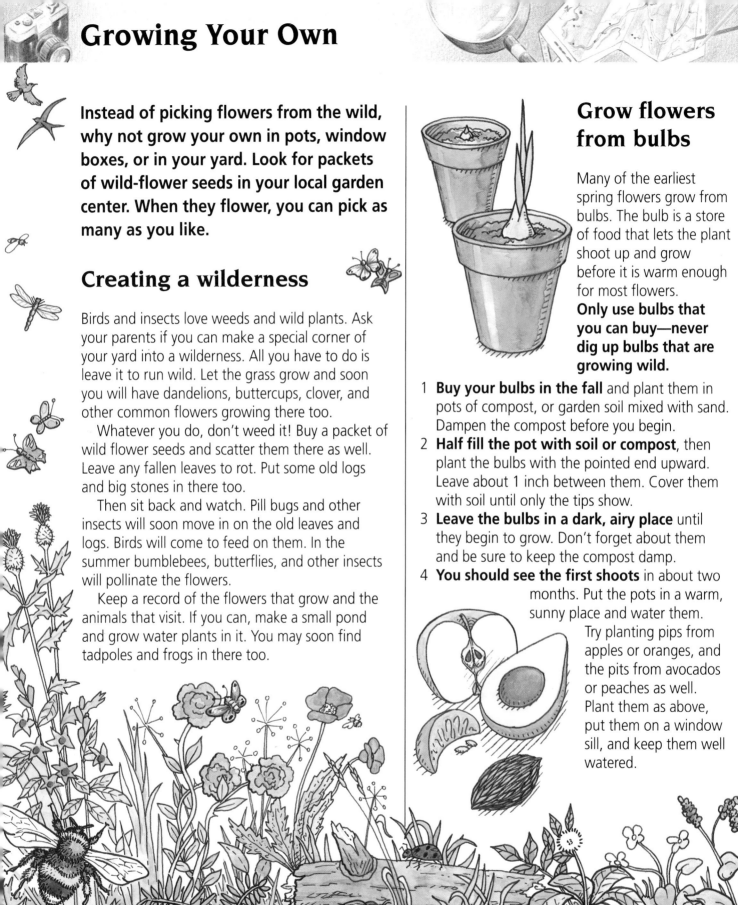

Hidden seeds

You can grow a surprise garden from the seeds you pick up on your sneakers on a muddy walk.

1 **Put on your sneakers and take a walk** after rain. It doesn't matter where you go, as long as it's muddy.

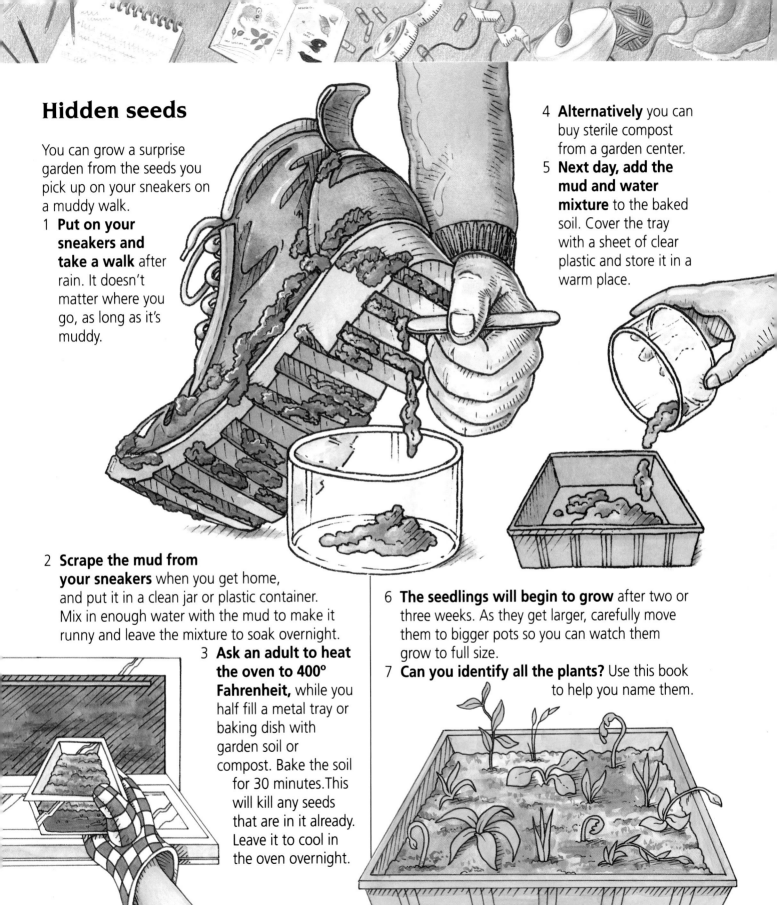

2 **Scrape the mud from your sneakers** when you get home, and put it in a clean jar or plastic container. Mix in enough water with the mud to make it runny and leave the mixture to soak overnight.

3 **Ask an adult to heat the oven to 400° Fahrenheit,** while you half fill a metal tray or baking dish with garden soil or compost. Bake the soil for 30 minutes. This will kill any seeds that are in it already. Leave it to cool in the oven overnight.

4 **Alternatively** you can buy sterile compost from a garden center.

5 **Next day, add the mud and water mixture** to the baked soil. Cover the tray with a sheet of clear plastic and store it in a warm place.

6 **The seedlings will begin to grow** after two or three weeks. As they get larger, carefully move them to bigger pots so you can watch them grow to full size.

7 **Can you identify all the plants?** Use this book to help you name them.

Western Forests

Most western forests are made up of evergreen trees with needle-like leaves, like pines, spruces, and firs. Different kinds of forest have different wild flowers growing in them. With a little practice, you will learn which flowers you could expect to find in a lodgepole pine forest, an Engelman spruce forest, a ponderosa pine forest, and so on.

Some western forests have deciduous trees, like aspen. Here, as in Eastern Forests (see pages 8–17), you will find most flowers in spring, when sunlight can warm the soil before the new leaves emerge.

Which trees and flowers grow in a forest depends on the amount of rain and sunshine ihe forest receives. Damp air from the Pacific Ocean blows across the mountains and valleys from west to east. The western sides of the mountain slopes are wetter than the eastern slopes. In some places the eastern mountainsides may be too dry for trees to grow at all—there is grassland and then desert.

Mountainsides that face south get more sun. So you are most likely to find trees and flowers that like a cool, wet environment on the northwestern side of a mountain, and those that like very warm and dry conditions on the southeastern side. This picture shows seven plants from this book. How many can you recognize?

Orange Agoseris, Blue Columbine, Yellow Faun Lily, Northern Inside-out Flower, Kinnikinnick, Bush Penstemon, Western Shooting Star.

Tall Cinquefoil

Look for the cluster of white flowers growing at the top of a thick stem that grows upward. Each flower has five petals cupped in two sets of sepals. Look for the other set of sepals below the real sepals. Feel the leaves and stem. They are covered with sticky, brown hairs. The leaves are divided into seven to eleven toothed, oval leaflets.

Rose family
Up to 3 ft tall – Flowers in May-August
Also grows in grasslands and is found farther east to Arizona

Large-flowered Brickelbush

Look for this plant in rocky places. The nodding flower heads are pale yellow or greenish, and grow in clusters on short stalks from the base of a leaf. They look like the center of daisies cupped in green and yellow, striped bracts. Look for the triangular leaves that grow in pairs up the stem, too.

Sunflower or Daisy family
Up to 3 ft tall
Flowers in August-September
Also grows on cliffs and mountainsides

Richardson's Cranesbill

Look for this plant in damp woods. It grows from a clump of leaves, each of which is deeply cut into five to seven sections. The flowers are white or pinkish and have purple veins. Look for the fruits when the flowers have died. Each fruit has five spoon-shaped sections with a seed in the bowl of each "spoon." When the seeds are ripe, the spoon handles contract and pull the bowls upward, throwing out the seeds.

Geranium family
About 1–3 ft tall
Flowers in June-August
Also grows in meadows

Miner's Lettuce

This unusual-looking plant likes damp and shady places. At the end of each flowering stem is a broad bowl-shaped disk, formed from two leaves that have joined together around the stem. In the center of each disk is a cluster of small, white flowers. Look for the clumps of spoon-shaped leaves. They are rich in vitamin C and gold miners used to eat them like lettuce.

Purslane family
Up to 1 ft tall
Flowers in March-June

Northern Inside-out Flower

You will easily recognize the strange shape of this flower. Both the white petals and sepals are swept back so that the flowers look like they are inside-out. The leaves are divided into groups of three leaflets, each with three lobes. They grow from underground rhizomes and form a slow-spreading carpet on the shady forest floor.

Barberry family
20 ins tall at most – Flowers in May-July

Western Rattlesnake Plantain

The easiest way to recognize this flower is by its leaves. They grow around the base of the stem, and have white veins that makes them look like snakeskin. The whitish flowers grow in a spike at the end of the stem. Each flower has a hood-like upper lip and a cupped lower lip.

Orchid family
Up to 1–3 ft tall
Flowers in July-September

Orange Agoseris

This plant looks a lot like a dandelion except that its flowers are a striking burnt-orange instead of yellow. Watch for them as they get older and turn purple or deep pinkish. Orange Agoseris is one of about ten Mountain Dandelions. Like real dandelions they have long, toothed leaves and flower stems full of milky juice.

Sunflower or Daisy family
6–24 ins tall – Flowers in June-August

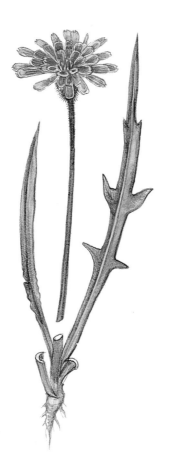

Heartleaf Arnica

Look for large patches of Heartleaf Arnica in open woods. It has one, two, or three yellow flower heads growing at the end of the stems. Look for the pairs of heart-shaped leaves, too. Like European Arnica, this plant has been used in herbal medicine to treat bruises and strains, but it can irritate the skin. It is poisonous if eaten.

Sunflower or Daisy family
Up to 2 ft tall – Flowers in April-June

Nuttall's Violet

Also known as the Yellow Prairie Violet, these yellow flowers have five petals, often tinged with purple on the outside. Look for the brownish purple veins on the petals. The flowers look a lot like the Downy Yellow Violet (see page 12), but their leaves are very different. They are lance-shaped or oval.

Violet family
1–3 ins tall – Flowers in April-July
Also grows in grasslands

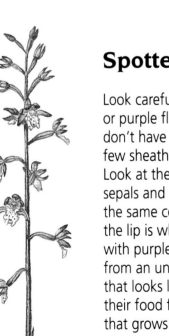

Spotted Coralroot

Look carefully at these yellowish or purple flowering stalks. They don't have any leaves, only a few sheaths near their base. Look at the flowers, too. Their sepals and side petals are almost the same color as the stalk, but the lip is whitish and spotted with purple. Coral-roots grow from an underground rhizome that looks like coral. They get their food from a special fungus that grows with them.

Orchid family
10–32 ins tall
Flowers in April-September

Yellow Fawn Lily

Yellow Fawn Lily is one of the first flowers you might see. It blooms as the snow begins to melt. It grows from corms (food-rich underground stems) and forms large patches of many plants. Look for the two oval or lance-shaped leaves at the base of each stem and for one to five nodding yellow flowers. Fawn Lilies are also called Adder's-tongues from the way the stamens flick out from the petals that are swept back.

Lily family
6–12 ins tall – Flowers in March-August
Also found on grassy slopes and grown in gardens

Sky Rocket

Sky Rocket has lots of other names —they all tell you something about it. Skunkflower gets its name from its slight smell of skunk, while Scarlet Gilia and Foxfire get their names from the color of the flowers. They are usually bright red, mottled with yellow, but can be pink. Desert Trumpet gets its name from the way the petals form a tube bent back at the ends. The leaves are deeply dissected into narrow segments, and grow mostly lower on the stems.

Phlox family
1–7 ft tall
Flowers in May–September
Also grows in scrub and chaparral, and in yards

Golden-beard Penstemon

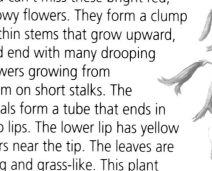

You can't miss these bright red, showy flowers. They form a clump of thin stems that grow upward, and end with many drooping flowers growing from them on short stalks. The petals form a tube that ends in two lips. The lower lip has yellow hairs near the tip. The leaves are long and grass-like. This plant is also known as Southwestern Penstemon.

Snapdragon or Figwort family
Up to 3 ft tall – Flowers in June–September
Also grown in yards

Kinnikinnick

Kinnikinnick is the Native American name for this plant. Europeans call it Bearberry. It is a woody, shrubby plant that grows close to the ground and often covers large areas. Look for the pink, bell-shaped flower. They are followed by bright red berries. Look for the spoon-shaped evergreen leaves, too. The Native Americans used to smoke them like tobacco. They were also  used for tanning leather.

Heath family
Creeping stem up to 10 ft long and 6 ins tall
Flowers in March–June
Grows in sandy and rocky ground

Western Shooting Star

You can't mistake this unusual and beautiful flower. Look for the drooping clusters of magenta flowers. Each has white bands and is shaped like a dart. See how the stamens are joined together and form a beak and the petals are swept back. The flower stem grows from a rosette of lance-shaped or oval leaves.

Primrose family
6–24 ins tall
Flowers in May–September
Also found on grassland, coasts, and in yards

Mission Bells

You will see how these flowers all look checkered, although they vary in color from purple-brown mottled with yellow, to lemon-yellow mottled with brownish purple. They are shaped like bowls and hang on arching stems from the base of the leaves. The leaves are lance-shaped and grow in whorls of three to five leaves. The thin stems grow upward from small bulbs. The plant is also known as Checker Lily.

Lily family
Up to 4 ft tall – Flowers in March-April
Also grows in scrub

Pipsissewa

Look for these waxy, fragrant flowers in early and middle of summer. Four to eight white or pinkish flowers hang from the top of each stem. They each have five petals and ten stamens with dark pink or red anthers. The narrow leaves are toothed and leathery, and grow in whorls on the stem. The plant was used by many Native Americans as a herbal remedy for rheumatism and kidney complaints.

Wintergreen family
Up to 1 ft tall – Flowers in June-August
Also grows in forests in southern Canada and much of the US

Giant Hyssop

This flower is easy to see because of the thick spike of flowers that grow at the end of the stems that grow upward. See how the flower head is made up of whorls of pale pink or lavender flowers, and how the stamens stick out beyond the flowers. The leaves look a lot like nettles—another name for the plant is Nettleleaf Horsemint.

Mint family
Up to 5 ft (150 cm) tall
Flowers in June-August

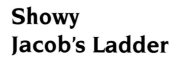

Showy Jacob's Ladder

This plant gets its names from its leaves. Each has several 11 to 23 pale green leaflets arranged in pairs opposite to each other so that they look like a ladder. Crush one so you can smell its skunk-like scent. The flowers grow in clusters at the end of the stems. They are blue, with yellow throats, and are shaped like a bowl.

Phlox family
2–12 ins tall – Flowers in May-August
Grows all over the higher western mountains

Western Monkshood

Monkshoods are easy to recognize. Make sure you don't touch them because they are very poisonous. Lots of showy, blue-violet flowers grow on each stem. The sepals look like petals and the top one forms a helmet-shaped hood over the flower. The large leaves are toothed and deeply lobed.

Buttercup or Crowfoot family
Up to 6 ft tall – Flowers in June-August
Also grows in high meadows

Western Dog Violet

The flowers of Western Dog Violet vary in color from pale to dark violet. They have five petals and the upper two are bent upward. Look for the backward spur on the lowest petal. Look at the leaves, too. They are rounded and scalloped around the edge. The stalk is long and erect.

Violet family
Up to 8 ins tall
Flowers in March-July
Also found in meadows
and on hillsides

Blue Columbine

Blue Columbine is the state flower of Colorado. It is easy to recognize because of its large, blue sepals and scoop-shaped, white petals which extend backward into hollow, blue claws. They hold the nectar. The flowers are followed by clusters of five segmented pods. The leaves are delicate and compound with deeply lobed leaflets, and grow in clumps.

Buttercup or Crowfoot family
Up to 3 ft tall
Flowers in May-August
Grows in the Rocky Mountains

Blue-pod Lupin

You will easily spot these long thick flower heads. Most of them are violet or blue, but some have reddish flowers. Notice how the sides of the petals are bent back giving the typical pea-like flower that yields to pods of seeds. The leaves are large, compound, and palmate, with leaflets arranged almost like spokes on a wagon wheel. This is the only lupin to grow in damp, lush places. Yard lupins have been developed from it.

Pea and Bean family
Up to 5 ft tall
Flowers in June-August
Also grows in damp meadows and next to streams

Bush Penstemon

This low-growing, shrubby plant forms thick patches of branching woody stems. Look for the showy lavender flowers and the pairs of lance-shaped leaves. Many flowers grow on each stem. The five petals join together to form a long tube with a two-lobed upper lip and a three-lobed lower lip, that flares out at the end.

Snapdragon or Figwort family
No more than 15 ins tall
Flowers in June-August
Grows on damp, rocky slopes; also grown in rock gardens

Experiments with Plants

Everyone knows plants need water and light, or they will die. They take in water through their roots from the soil. But how does the water flow up from the roots to every other part of the plant? Also, perform experiments to show plants turning to the light, and making water and oxygen.

Coloring a flower

This experiment shows how stems move water from the roots to the leaves and flowers.

1 **Take a white flower**—like a carnation, geranium, or Queen Anne's Lace (see page 65)—and carefully split the lower part of its stem into two.
2 **Fill two small pots with water.** Color one with red food dye and the other with blue or another color.
3 **Put one half of the stem** in one pot and the other half in the other pot. Leave it for an hour or two, or overnight.
4 **What happens to the flower?** Look at the split stem to see the tiny tubes, or "xylem," now colored by the dyed water.

You can use any food dye you like in these pots. Or you could mix two colors together (red and blue, for example, to make purple). But be careful—don't spill any on your clothes!

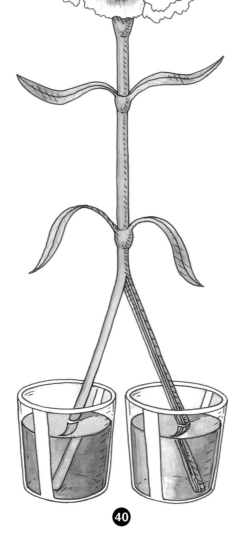

Plants lose water, too

Plants breathe just like we do. They take in oxygen from the air through tiny holes in their leaves called "stomata." Plants need both oxygen and food to grow. As the oxygen and sugar (food) are broken down, they give off carbon dioxide and water, which leave through the stomata.

1 **Take a small potted plant** and water it well.
2 **Put a clear plastic bag over all the leaves.** Make sure your bag is large enough that it doesn't squash the leaves, then tie it firmly around the base of the stem.
3 **Leave it in a sunny spot.**
4 **After an hour or two** the inside of the bag will be covered with little drops of water which the plant has breathed out.

Striped celery

Do the same experiment with a stick of celery. When you cut across the stem, the red dots show the "xylem", or tiny tubes that carry water and nutrients up from the roots.

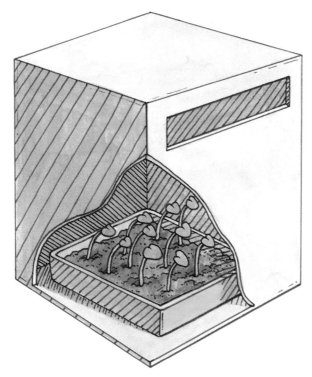

Light tease

Plants turn their leaves and grow toward the light. Put a potted plant near a window and in a day or so you will see that all its leaves are facing the light. Then turn it round. How long does it take for the leaves to turn to face the light again?

Most plants grow fairly straight up toward the light, but what happens if the light is coming only from one side?

1 **Take a large cardboard box** and cut a wide slit out of the bottom of one side (see the picture).
2 **Plant up a pot or tray of quick-growing seedlings**, like bean sprouts or sunflowers.
3 **Put the box over the seedlings** so that no light gets in except from the slit.
4 **Put the whole experiment in a sunny place** with the slit facing the sun and leave it for a few days. What happens to the seedlings?
5 **You can tease them** by turning them around to face away from the slit. Put the box back in the sun and see what happens in the next few days.

Make an oxygen bubble

While leaves are making food, they also make oxygen. In fact, much of the oxygen we breathe from the air has been made by plants. This experiment will show you this happening.

1 **Buy a few aquatic plants** from a pet store that sells tropical fish.
2 **Fill an aquarium or a large glass or clear plastic container** with water and put the plants in the bottom. Put it in a sunny place.
3 **Cut off the top of a large, clear plastic bottle**, take off its screw cap, and place it over the plants.
4 **Balance a small glass over the top of the bottle** as shown in the picture. Make sure there is no air in the glass by holding it under water first.
5 **After a few days** you should notice a space at the top of the glass where the oxygen is collecting. You may even see bubbles rising from the plant.

Wetlands

This habitat includes marshes, swamps, wet woods, and ditches in addition to the banks and sides of ponds and streams. You will even find some of these flowers growing in shallow water providing it is still or slow-moving.

Most wetlands are free of trees and get lots of sunshine. The flowers that bloom here usually need lots of direct sunlight and most bloom in the late spring and summer. Those that grow in swamps, however, have to cope with shade. They bloom earlier in the spring or make do with less light.

All plants need water, but to survive in these wet conditions the plants have to adapt in special ways. To prevent them from becoming water-logged, plants that grow in shallow water, like water lilies, have glossy, waterproof leaves and flowers. Most wetland plants have special air ducts in their leaves and stems to carry oxygen from the air to the parts of the plant growing underneath the surface.

Very wet soil is not as fertile as drier ground. Minerals and nutrients are easily washed away. The Purple Gerardia overcomes this problem by taking nourishment from the roots of grass onto which it clings. Water lilies take advantage of the water to disperse their seeds. This picture shows seven plants from this book. How many can you recognize?

Arrowhead, Cattail, Blue Flag, Joe-pye Weed, Marsh Marigold, Turtlehead, Fragrant Water Lily

Wetlands

Fragrant Water Lily

This beautiful, white flower floats on quiet waters and ponds and opens in the morning to show its many yellow stamens. The floating leaves are round, and grow on long stalks from a stem or rhizome under the mud at the bottom of the pond. As the flower dies, its long stalk coils back under the surface so that the seed capsule ripens under water. When it bursts, the seeds rise to the surface and float away.

Water Lily family
Flowers up to 8 ins above the water
Flowers in May-July

Ragged Fringed Orchid

This plant grows in open swamps, bogs, wet woods, and meadows, and in marshes in the eastern half of Canada and the US. The flowers are creamy-yellow or greenish yellow. If you look closely you can see that the lip of each is divided into three lobes, each one deeply cut to form a fringe. The leaves are lance-shaped and grow on the lower part of the stem that grows upward.

Orchid family
2–3 ft tall
Flowers in June-September

Giant Helleborine

These showy flowers grow next to lakes, springs, and streams in the western US, and form colonies of leafy stems that grow upward. Their leaves are large and lance-shaped or oval. The flowers are purple-veined, and grow from the base of the leaves. The sepals are greenish brown. The pinkish or purplish petals are shorter. The purple lip is spoon-shaped with a salmon-pink tongue.

Orchid family
Up to 3 ft tall – Flowers in March-August

Common Cattail

This plant is easy to recognize from the long cylinder of brown flowers or seeds growing on thick stems with stiff, sword-like leaves. It grows in marshes, and next to ponds and slow-moving rivers. A spike of tiny, yellow, male flowers grow at the top of the stem above the brownish, female flowers. The male flowers fade and disappear soon after shedding their pollen, leaving a bare stalk. The female flowers develop into brown seeds with a fluffy appearance when pulled apart. The rootstock was eaten by Native Americans and early colonists. It is also a favorite food of muskrats.

Cattail family
Up to 9 ft tall – Flowers in May-October

Arrowhead

This plant grows in marshes and ditches, and next to lakes and slow-moving rivers. The arrowhead-shaped leaves are easy to recognize and give the plant its name. The many white or pale pink flowers grow in whorls near the top of the long, flowering stem. The plant is also called Duck Potato because of the potato-like swellings on its root. They were a valuable food to the Native Americans and you can still collect them between late summer and spring.

Water Plantain family
Up to 4 ft tall
Flowers in May-August

Turtlehead

Look for the thick cluster of white flowers growing at the end of the stem. They grow in wet places in the eastern US. Each flower has two lips and looks like a turtle's head. Look at the leaves, too. They are narrow and toothed, and grow in opposite pairs up the stiff stem.

Snapdragon or
Figwort family
1–3 ft tall
Flowers in
July-September

Lizard's Tail

This plant grows in shallow water, swamps, and marshes in the eastern half of Canada and the US. It gets its name from the tiny, white flowers. They form long spikes, which droop at the tips like a lizard's tail. Look for the large, dark leaves, too. They are heart-shaped and are 3–6 inches long. The flowers are followed by juicy capsules.

Lizard's Tail family
Up to 5 ft tall
Flowers in May-July

Boneset

You may first see the spreading masses of white flower heads, but the best way to identify Boneset is from its leaves. They are large, lance-shaped, wrinkled, and opposite to each other. The pair are joined so that the stem seems to grow through them. The hairy stems grow together in clumps. It grows in low, wet places in the eastern half of Canada and the US. Boneset has long been used by the Native Americans, and later by the settlers, in herbal medicine as a tonic. The Native Americans used it to treat fevers associated with colds, influenza, and malaria, before the invention of modern drugs.

Sunflower or Daisy flower
2–4 ft tall – Flowers in August-October

Canada Lily

This beautiful plant grows in the eastern US in wet meadows and next to the edge of woods. It is also called Wild Yellow Lily and Meadow Lily. Its drooping flowers are yellow or yellow-orange and marked with purplish brown spots. The petals overlap to form a funnel, then arch backward at the end. The leaves are lance-shaped, and grow in whorls of between four and ten leaves.

Lily family
Up to 5 ft tall – Flowers in June-August

Yellow-eyed Grass

Look for this grass beside ponds and ditches, in sandy swamps, and wet pine-barrens, but only in the southeastern US. It forms a clump of straight leaves with yellow flowers at the end of long, leafless stalks. The flowers rise from a cone of woody bracts which hides the buds and fruits. Each has three petals and three sepals. One sepal is hooded and soon drops off. The other two are boat-shaped or winged.

Yellow-eyed Grass family
Up to 3 ft tall
Flowers in July-September

Marsh Marigold

Look for these showy, yellow flowers in marshes, wet meadows, and thickets, and next to streams. The flowers have five to nine petals and as many as 100 stamens. Their stalks are hollow. The large, dark green leaves are heart-shaped and grow in clumps. Look for their toothed edges and long stalks, too.

Buttercup or Crowfoot family
Up to 2 ft tall
Flowers in April-May

Swamp Candles

This plant grows in open swamps and wet places in the eastern US. These bright yellow flowers form big, candle-like spikes. Look for the red spots on the petals. The leaves are opposite to each other and are canoe-shaped. Swamp Candles produce special buds at the base of the leaves. As the plant dies in the winter, these buds drop to the ground and form new plants in the spring.

Primrose family
Up to 3 ft tall
Flowers in June-August

Seep-Spring Monkey-flower

This plant grows all over the Rocky Mountains. For most of the year it covers the ground with a mat of creeping, overlapping stems. Then in the summer it sends up shoots with pairs of rounded leaves and yellow flowers spotted with orange. Look closely at one of the flowers. It has two broad lips which join to form a funnel. The upper lip has two lobes and the lower lip has three.

Snapdragon or Figwort family
Up to 3 ft tall
Flowers in March-September

Sneezeweed

This plant grows in wet meadows, marshes, and ditches. It has lots of yellow flower heads at the ends of the stem. They have greenish yellow disk flowers in the center surrounded by yellow ray flowers. These bend backward, so that they look like round buttons with streamers attached to them. The toothed leaves are lance-shaped, and look like wings attached to the stems. This plant was used to make snuff, to make people sneeze.

Sunflower or Daisy family
Up to 5 ft tall – Flowers in July-October
Also grown in yards

Pale Touch-me-not

This plant grows in wet, shady places in meadows and woods. The drooping, pale yellow flowers grow on long, arching stems from the base of the leaves. They have yellow petals and sepals which look like petals. Look closely and you might see a few red-brown spots on the yellow. The leaves are toothed and egg-shaped, and alternate up the stem. The flowers are replaced by green seed-pods that burst when ripe and spread their seeds if you touch them. This plant is not as common as Spotted Touch-me-not (see page 49.)

Touch-me-not family
3–6 ft tall
Flowers in June-October

Yellow Water Lily

These yellow, bowl-shaped flowers grow in ponds and slow-moving streams in the western US. They float on the water's surface or stand up above the water. The plant has two kinds of leaf: waxy, oval, notched leaves which float on the surface, and thin, delicate ones under the water. The flowers are followed by egg-shaped fruits that ripen above the surface and burst to release the seeds. They can be roasted like popcorn or ground into meal.

Water Lily family
Flowers 1–3 ins above water
Flowers in April-September

Wetlands

Checkermallow

These narrow, flowering spikes are crowded with deep pink flowers. They grow from a clump of round leaves with shallow lobes. Leaves higher up the stem are deeply divided into seven palmate lobes. They grow next to streams, ponds, springs, and in wet places on the lower slopes of the Rocky Mountains. Many kinds of Checkermallow are also grown as yard plants.

Mallow family
Up to 3 ft tall
Flowers in June-September

Rose Pogonia

You will easily recognize this flower but you will be lucky to find it because it is quite rare. It grows in bogs in eastern Canada and the US. The fragrant, pink flower has three pink sepals which look like petals, and two petals which arch over a flat lip. The lip is fringed and bearded with short, yellow and pink bristles. Each stem has one lance-shaped or oval leaf part of the way up. It is also sometimes called Snake-mouth.

Orchid family
Up to 2 ft tall
Flowers in May-June

Cardinal Flower

You can't miss these spikes of brilliant red flowers. They grow in wet places in the eastern half of the US. Look closely at one of the two-lipped flowers. The upper lip stands up, but the lower one droops and spreads into three lobes. The leaves are narrow and toothed, and alternate up the stems that grow upward.

Bellflower or Bluebell family
2–4 ft tall – Flowers in July-September

Common Meadow Beauty

This plant grows in bogs, damp meadows, and wet pinelands in the eastern and southern US. You will easily recognize the flower because of its four, large, pink petals and yellow stamens. Look for the fruit capsules which follow the flowers. They flare out at the neck and look like urns. The leaves are egg-shaped, and have almost no stalks. They grow in opposite pairs up the stem.

Meadow Beauty family
1–2 ft tall
Flowers in July-September

Spotted Touch-me-not

Look for this plant next to streams and springs, and in damp woods. Its large flowers are helmet-shaped and hang in small clusters on long, arching stems from the base of the leaves. They are orange-yellow with red-brown spots. They are followed by capsules that burst open at the slightest touch. The stems are translucent and ooze a watery juice if broken. This juice and that of Pale Touch-me-not (see page 47,) relieves the itching of poison ivy.

Touch-me-not family
Up to 5 ft tall
Flowers in June-October

Red Iris

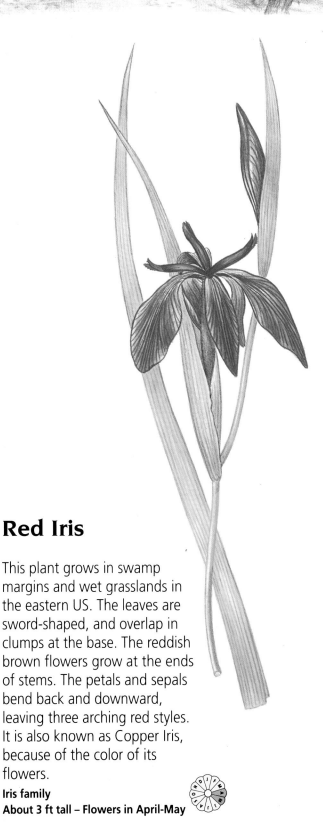

This plant grows in swamp margins and wet grasslands in the eastern US. The leaves are sword-shaped, and overlap in clumps at the base. The reddish brown flowers grow at the ends of stems. The petals and sepals bend back and downward, leaving three arching red styles. It is also known as Copper Iris, because of the color of its flowers.

Iris family
About 3 ft tall – Flowers in April-May

Wetlands

Blue Flag

Look for clumps of these violet or blue-violet flowers in the East in marshes, wet meadows, and on shores of ponds. The drooping sepals are darker blue. They are marked with yellow and white with deep purple veins at the center. The three petals stand up. The overlapping, sword-shaped leaves sometimes stand up and sometimes arch. They grow from underground stems called rhizomes. These are poisonous like those of many irises.

Iris family
Up to 3 ft tall
Flowers in May-August

Purple Loosestrife

You will easily spot large clumps of these pinkish purple flowers growing next to streams, lakes, and in marshes, wet meadows, and roadside ditches in the late summer. Look closely at the flower spikes and you will see that they are made up of whorls of many flowers, each with six crumpled petals. The leaves are lance-shaped, and grow in opposite pairs.

Loosestrife family
2–4 ft tall – Flowers in May-July

Joe-pye Weed

These fuzzy, purple flower heads look like Ironweed, but they form more tightly packed, flat-topped clusters. Look for the lance-shaped, toothed leaves which grow in whorls of three to five leaves. See how the stout stems are streaked and spotted with purple. It grows in damp meadows, thickets, and on the banks of ponds.

Sunflower or Daisy family
Up to 6 ft tall
Flowers in June-August

Square-stemmed Monkey-flower

In the eastern US, this flower grows next to streams and in marshes. It doesn't grow in western states. Look for the pairs of lance-shaped leaves and the blue flowers. Each flower has two lips with yellow at the center. Look for the square-shaped stem, too. The flowers are followed by capsules of seeds.

Snapdragon or Figwort family
1–3 ft tall
Flowers in June-September

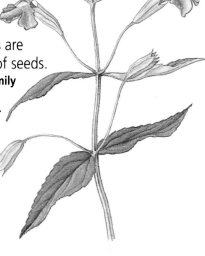

Purple Gerardia

Growing on shores and in bogs, each of these pink flowers lasts only for one day. They are shaped a little bit like bells, and grow in clusters at the ends of the wiry stems. The leaves are small and narrow and grow in opposite pairs. The plant is semi-parasitic as it gets some of its food by attaching itself to the roots of grasses.

Snapdragon or Figwort family
1–4 ft tall
Flowers in July-September

American Brooklime

This plant grows in marshes and next to streams except in the far South. The fleshy stems root in the mud, then creep and sprawl under the mud and send up stems. Look for the open, oblong clusters of blue flowers which grow from the base of the upper leaves. The leaves are lance-shaped, and grow in pairs along the stems.

Snapdragon or Figwort family
Up to 3 ft tall
Flowers in May-July

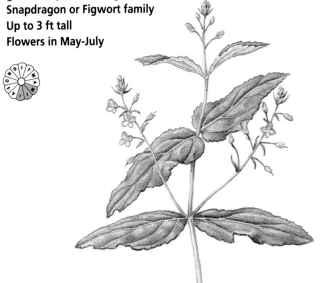

Woundwort

These purple flowers grow in whorls at the base of the upper leaves. Each flower has two lips. The upper one forms a hood, and the lower one is marked with white. The leaves are lance-shaped with jagged edges, and grow in pairs up the stem. It grows in damp places and marshes. Woundwort is an antiseptic and was traditionally used to tie wounds. It supposedly stopped bleeding and helped the wound to heal.

Mint family
Up to 3 ft tall
Flowers in
July-September

New York Ironweed

This plant has lots of purple or deep lavender flower heads and grows in low, wet places and on streambanks in parts of the eastern US. The toothed, lance-shaped leaves alternate up the erect stems. At one time Ironweeds were used in herbal medicine to stimulate the appetite and help digestion.

Sunflower or Daisy family
3–6 ft tall
Flowers in August-October

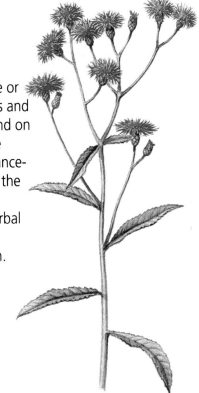

Preserving Wild Flowers

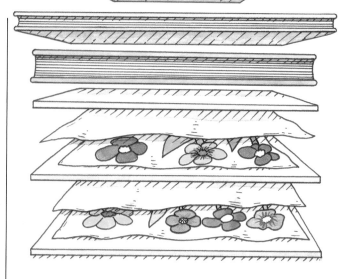

Most wild flowers soon wither if you pick them, but you can preserve them for a long time by pressing or drying them. Chose only flowers that you know are common, and do not pick them unless there are lots of them. Remember to pick a stem with a leaf, or take a separate leaf to press with it.

Flat flower heads like buttercups, violets, Blue Columbine, Wild Flax, and Prairie Star press well. Avoid very bulky flower heads like Red Clover, sunflowers, or Teasel. It is better to dry those. Take a plastic bag to put the flowers in. It will help to keep them fresh until you get home.

1 **Arrange the flowers and leaves carefully** on the sheets of paper towel. Give each flower enough room, and remember it will press dry just as you have arranged it.

2 **Start with a piece of cardboard** or four layers of folded newspaper on a flat, hard surface. Lay a paper towel with flowers on top of it. Put another sheet of paper towel and then cardboard or folded newspaper on top of it.

3 **Go on adding layers of flowers** between paper towels and cardboard or newspaper until you have a stack no more than 6 inches high. Finish with a cardboard or newspaper layer.

4 **Carefully place the heavy books on top of the stack.**

5 **Leave the flowers alone for two weeks.** Then peel the paper back gently and check that the flowers are flat and dried. If they are not, leave them for another week.

Pressing flowers

You can buy a flower press ready-made, or you can make your own. You will need paper towels, cardboard or newspaper, and several heavy books. You can use out-of-date telephone directories or any heavy books like encyclopedias. Choose a warm, dry room to make your press, and a table or cupboard where it can remain undisturbed for two or three weeks.

Drying flowers

Drying is even better than pressing for preserving wild flowers. It keeps their shape as well as their color, and in some cases dried flowers are hard to tell from fresh ones.

Members of the daisy family, like daisies, thistles, and dandelions all dry well. Thistles, Field Scabious, and roses are good too. Always pick the flowers just before they are in full bloom.

Don't pick any flowers that are beginning to fade or wither, unless of course you wait until they go to seed. Poppies, Teasel, and many other seed heads look very attractive dried. So do grasses.

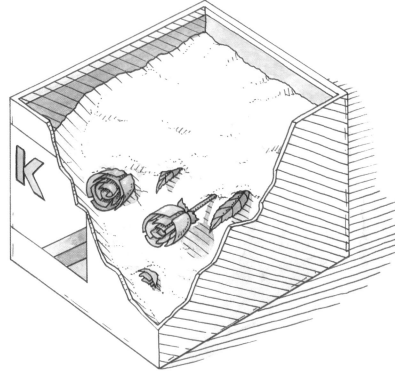

Air drying

The easiest way to dry flowers is by tying them into a bunch with a rubber band, then hanging them upside-down in a dry, airy place for a few weeks. A linen cupboard is ideal because you can hang them up easily. An attic, spare room, or garage is also fine, but you will need to fix up a pole or line to hang them from. Don't put more than 8–10 stems into each bunch.

Drying more delicate flowers

Some flowers lose some of their shape and color if they are just air-dried. It's better to dry roses, lilies, and anemones using a mixture of cornmeal and borax, which you can buy from a supermarket or grocery store. This way preserves leaves better too.

1 **Find a box,** like a shoe box, which is large enough to hold the flowers easily.
2 **Mix equal parts of borax and cornmeal** together, enough to half fill the box.
3 **Pour some of the mixture into the box** to make a layer 1 inch deep.
4 **Cut the flower stems** so that they fit into the box, and carefully arrange the flowers on top of the mixture without overlapping each other.
5 **Gently sprinkle some more of the mixture over the flowers** until they are covered by a layer about 1 inch deep.
6 **After a week,** gently take the flowers from the box and dust off the drying mixture with an artist's paintbrush.

Deserts

The best word to describe a desert is dry since deserts have less rain than anywhere else on Earth. And it is not hard to recognize a desert. If less than half the undisturbed ground is covered by plants, you are probably in a desert.

Desert plants have special ways of overcoming these extremely dry and often hot conditions. Plants usually lose water through their leaves, so the leaves of cacti have become no more than spikes. They store water inside their round, swollen stems that gives less surface for water to evaporate from. Other plants have long roots that grow close to the surface to catch as much moisture as possible.

The seeds of desert wild flowers sprout only when the rain comes which, in North American deserts, is just once or twice a year. Then the seeds grow very quickly in the damp soil, and for a short while the desert looks like it is covered with blooms. By the time the dry weather returns, they have produced their seeds, which lie waiting for the next rainy season. This picture shows seven plants from this book. How many can you recognize?

Claret Cup Cactus, Tangled Fishhook Cactus, Desert Lily, Climbing Milkweed, Desert Mountain Phlox, California Poppy, Broom Snakeweed

Tree Cholla

This cactus forms a shrub or small tree, with lots of low branches. When the branches die they stay on the plant, so old plants are a mass of dead stems and new, green ones. The stems have very long joints. Look for the many round swellings with clusters of 10 to 30 short, yellowish spines. The flowers are dark reddish lavender, or purple, and grow at the ends of the branches.

Cactus family
3–7 ft tall – Flowers in May-July
Also grows on plains and in
pinyon-juniper woodlands

Claret Cup Cactus

This beautiful cactus is also called a hedgehog cactus because it forms a low mound of round spiny stems. Each stem has deep ribs covered with clusters of spines. The bright scarlet flowers are shaped like claret glasses, and give the plant its name. They are followed by fat, red fruits.

Cactus family
2–12 ins tall
Flowers in April-May
Also grows in dry
mountain woods
and on rocky
slopes

Simpson's Ball Cactus

This cactus grows in clumps of ball-shaped stems. Each stem has 8 to 13 ribs with lots of spiny swellings. Each cluster of spines has 8 to 13 thick spines in the center with 10 to 25 thinner spines around them. The flowers are rose-purple, white, or yellow-green and grow near the top of the stem.

Cactus family
No more than 8 ins tall – Flowers in May-July
Also grows among sagebrush and pinyon-juniper woodlands

Tangled Fishhook Cactus

Fishhook cacti have one or more, round, single stems with tangled-looking spines. The central spine of each cluster is shaped like a fishhook and is surrounded by straight, overlapping spines. The deep pink flowers grow in the spaces between the clusters of spines, and are followed by smooth, red fruits.

Cactus family
Up to 6 ft tall
Flowers in May-June
Also grows in very
dry grassland

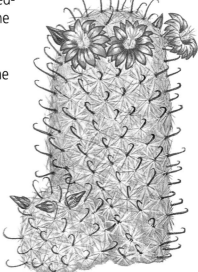

Deserts

Sulphur Flower

These bright yellow flowers grow in clusters at the tops of long stalks. Look for the clump of leaves at the end of each branch. They are spoon-shaped with long stalks. They are more or less hairless above, but covered with white hairs underneath.

Smartweed or Buckwheat family
4–12 ins tall
Flowers in June-August
Also grows on dry sunny areas from sagebrush deserts to tundra

Rabbit Brush

This shrub looks a lot like Broom Snakeweed. The yellow flower heads grow in thick clusters at the ends of the stems. It gives off a strong odour, however, and looks gray-white, because its stems are thickly covered with gray or white hairs. The leaves are up to 3 inches long.

Sunflower or Daisy family
Up to 7 ft tall
Flowers in August-October

Californian Poppy

This plant is the state flower of California and is one of the best-known poppies. It has clumps of ragged, blue-green leaves, divided into deep segments. The orange-yellow flowers grow on their own and open only in sunlight. They close at night, and stay closed on cloudy days.

Poppy family
Up to 2 ft tall
Flowers in February-October
Also grows on grasslands, hillsides, and in yards

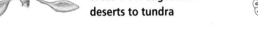

Threadleaf Groundsel

This plant grows in bushy clumps with branched stems and lots of yellow flower heads. The long, thin leaves are bluish green and covered in woolly hairs when they first grow. Threadleaf Groundsel also grows well on ranges, but cattle usually avoid it because it is poisonous.

Sunflower or Daisy family
1–3 ft tall – Flowers in June-August
Also grows on pinyon-juniper ranges and dry, rocky plains

Golden Prince's Plume

You can easily recognize this flower because of its long, spiky plumes of bright yellow flower heads. Look for the unusual shape of the small flowers. The yellow sepals bend backward as the flower opens and the four petals spread out, leaving the long stamens sticking far out of the flower. The flowers are followed by thin pods of seeds.

Mustard family
Up to 5 ft tall – Flowers in May-July

Yellow Bee Plant

This tall plant grows on sandy flats and scrub, often near water. Look for the compound, palmate leaves with three to seven leaflets and the yellow flowers clustered at the top of the stems. The lower flowers open first and are followed by slender pods of seeds on arched, jointed stalks. Despite their strong, goaty smell, the flowers are very attractive to bees, so giving the plant its name.

Caper family
Up to 5 ft tall – Flowers in May-September
Also found in juniper woodland

Broom Snakeweed

This plant has lots of flat-topped, yellow flower heads and thin, brittle stems. Look for the narrow leaves, and feel how sticky the plant is. As its name tells you, the plant is used by Native Americans as a remedy for snake bites. The stems can be tied together to make a broom, too.

Sunflower or Daisy family
Up to 3 ft tall
Flowers in August-September

Desert Gold

This tiny plant has funnel-shaped flowers which vary in color from pale to deep yellow. Look for the purple-brown on their throats. The leaves are spaced apart up the thin stems, and each one has three to seven needle-like segments.

Phlox family
Not more than 4 ins tall
Flowers in May-June

Deserts

Climbing Milkvine

Look for this vine twining in and around the branches of other bushes. The white, purplish, or pink flower heads are made up of tiny star-like flowers. Each has five petals and a furry fringe. The leaves grow in pairs and are lance-shaped or triangular.

Milkweed family
10 ft long
Flowers in April-August

Brown-eyes

Look for the brown spot at the base of each of the four white petals. They give the plant its name. Several flowers grow from the top of each stem. They become reddish as they get older. Look at the leaves, too. They are toothed, and grow in a rosette at the base of the stem.

Evening Primrose family
Up to 20 ins tall
Flowers in May-July

Desert Lily

You can easily recognize this plant from its clumps of distinctive-looking leaves. They are long and narrow with wavy, crinkled edges. The white lily-like flowers are shaped like funnels, and grow at the end of the flowering stem which grows upward.

Lily family
1–6 ft tall
Flowers in March-May

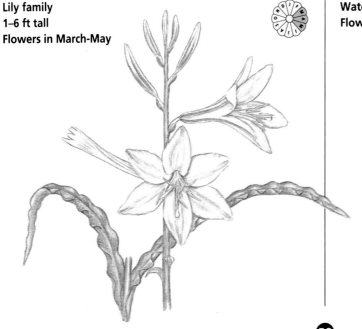

Wild Heliotrope

The flowers of this plant grow in curled clusters. They uncurl as they open into very large blue flowers shaped like bells. The stems can grow upward or sprawl along the ground. The leaves are divided and look almost like ferns.

Waterleaf family – 2–3 ft tall
Flowers in March-June – Also grows in fields

Desert Sand Verbena

This creeping plant has opposite, egg-shaped leaves and fragrant umbels of trumpet-shaped flowers. The flowers have rose-purple sepals that look like petals, and a white center. Feel the plant. It is covered with long, sticky hairs.

Four-o'clock family
10 ins high & 3 ft long
Flowers in March-October

Desert Anemone

The flowers of Desert Anemone can be white, rose pink, or pinkish purple, with yellow centers. The flowers don't have petals but this isn't very noticeable because the sepals look just like petals. Each flower grows at the end of a separate branch with a whorl of three divided leaves midway on the stem and more at the base. The plant has tuberous roots in which it stores food and water.

Buttercup or Crowfoot family
4–6 ins tall
Flowers in March-April

Desert Sage

You can recognize this plant because of the bright blue or blue-violet flower clusters and the silvery leaves. The clusters are made up of whorls of two-lipped flowers surrounded by purplish bracts. The stems are spiny and form a broad, low-growing shrub.

Mint family
8–30 ins tall
Flowers in May-July

Desert Mountain Phlox

This little tufted plant has lots of short branched stems which grow from a woody base. Its flowers have five petals and can be pink or white. The stems are thickly covered with narrow, gray-green, needle-like leaves. Rub them to see how strong they smell.

Phlox family
Up to 6 ins tall
Flowers in May-July
Also grows in
western mountains

Things to Make

A flower calendar

You can make a flower calendar to put on your bedroom wall.

1 **Buy a large sheet of paper from an art supplies store** and divide it up into twelve equal areas, or strips. Write the name of the months in the center of the strips.

2 **When you go for a walk**, make a note and a drawing of the flowers you see. If you have a camera, you could take a picture instead.

3 **Stick the photo or drawing onto the calendar** in the month you saw the flower.

4 **Alternatively, you can copy the picture** of the flower from this book and color it in yourself before adding it to your calendar. Or you can cut a picture of the flower out of a nature magazine.

For a more detailed record of the wild flowers you see, use a pad of plain paper. When you see a wild flower, make a drawing of it as shown (right). Write down the date you saw it and the place it was growing. Was it in bud, full flower, or in seed?

Use a new page for each kind of flower and leave space to add more notes from future walks. As your note pages build up, you can keep them in a ring binder.

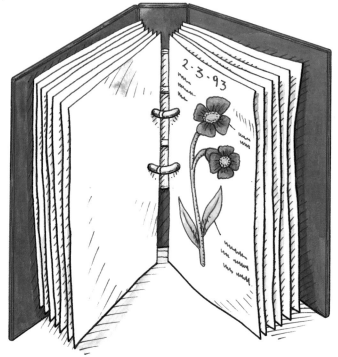

Bookmark gift

Tall thin flowers make good bookmarks. You will need one sheet of clear adhesive-backed plastic.

1 **Cut two pieces of the plastic**; make them a little bigger than you need the bookmark to be. Peel the backing off one piece and lay it sticky side up on a flat surface.

2 **Lay the pressed flower carefully on the sticky plastic.**

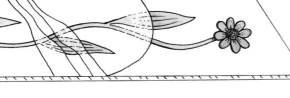

3 **Peel the backing off the other cut piece** and lay it carefully on top of the flower. The two pieces do not need to match up exactly.

4 **Draw the outline of the bookmark onto the plastic** with a ballpoint pen and cut around it through both layers of plastic. The flower will show clearly from both sides of the bookmark.

Flower pictures

You can use dried flowers or pressed flowers (see pages 52–53) to make a picture.

1 **Use a piece of thick paper,** like artist's paper or good quality writing paper. Paint a landscape as a background, if you like.

2 **Arrange the flowers in a pattern,** or place them as they would look if they were growing. Don't put the flowers too close to the edge if you are planning to frame your picture.

3 **When you are happy with the arrangement,** stick it down using small amounts of glue on the back of each flower and leaf.

4 **If you have used pressed flowers,** you can frame your picture behind glass. With dried flowers you will have to leave them uncovered.

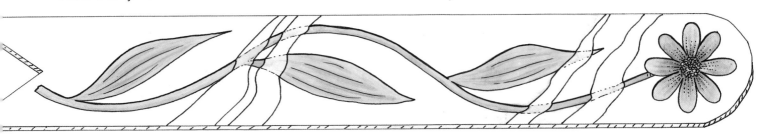

Roadsides & Parks

This habitat includes building sites, lawns and yards, waste ground, meadows, pastures, abandoned farm fields, and railroads. In fact it describes any place where the natural habitat has been disturbed or altered by human activity.

Many of the plants in this habitat are not native to North America. They have been brought here by people from other continents, mostly Europe and Asia. Some have escaped from yards, some from fields. This habitat gives flowers particular problems and the ones that have adapted to human activity over thousands of years are the ones that thrive.

Many disturbed habitats have little fertile topsoil. The plants that grow here have to make do with less nutrients than in other habitats. Instead they need plenty of direct sunlight to thrive. Agricultural land has plenty of topsoil but, like waste ground and building sites, the ground is only available for a short while. Plants that need a long time to established themselves can't do well here. Instead, plants that can put down roots, grow, flower, and set seed quickly, invade the land.

Many of these plants produce large numbers of seeds that can spread over a great distance. When the seeds land on an area of waste land, the cycle starts over again. The picture shows nine plants from this book. How many can you recognize?

Yarrow.
Common Morning Glory, Tansy, Bull Thistle,
Red Clover, White Clover, Ox-eye Daisy,
Lesser Burdock, Chicory,

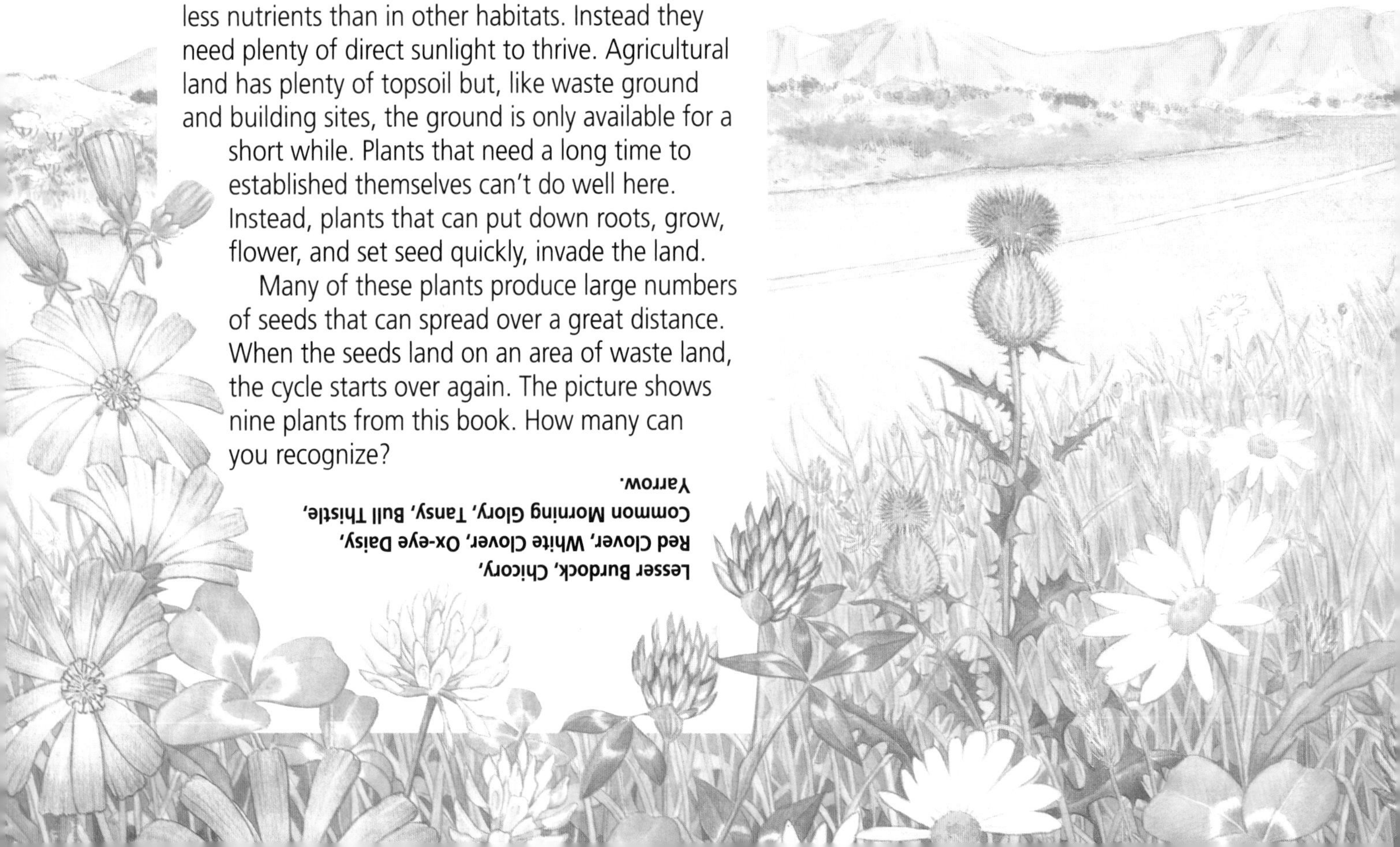

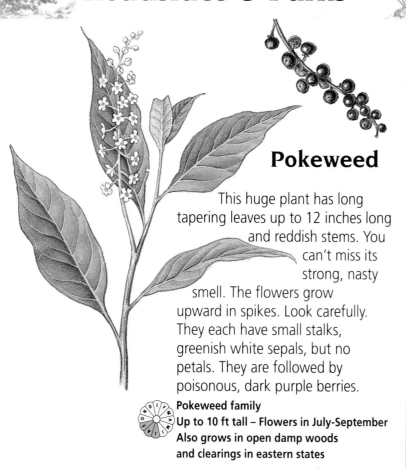

Pokeweed

This huge plant has long tapering leaves up to 12 inches long and reddish stems. You can't miss its strong, nasty smell. The flowers grow upward in spikes. Look carefully. They each have small stalks, greenish white sepals, but no petals. They are followed by poisonous, dark purple berries.

Pokeweed family
Up to 10 ft tall – Flowers in July-September
Also grows in open damp woods
and clearings in eastern states

Wild Strawberry

Wild strawberries are smaller, but sweeter and tastier, than cultivated strawberries. The white flowers have five, separate, round petals. Look into the center of the flower. The many pistils lead to a green cone, which will eventually swell to form the strawberry. If you look at a ripe strawberry you can see the seeds embedded on the outside.

Rose family
Creeping stem with
3–6 ins flower stalk
Flowers in April-June

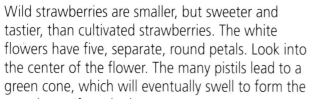

Daisy Fleabane

The narrow ray flowers of the Daisy Fleabane are usually white, but can be pink. They surround a wide, yellow center, and grow in clusters at the end of the leafy stems. The leaves are toothed and lance-shaped. Both leaves and stems are covered with spreading hairs. Many kinds of fleabane have been developed as yard flowers.

Sunflower or Daisy family
1–5 ft tall
Flowers in June-October
Also grows in yards and fields

Ox-eye Daisy

You can tell the Ox-eye Daisy apart from the other similar daisies because each stem has only one, large, daisy-like flower head. The ray flowers are white, and the central disk is yellow and has a depression in the middle. Look at the leaves, too. They are dark green and have deep cuts. Ox-eye Daisies often grow together in large colonies. As a yard plant, it has lots of other names, including Moon Daisy, Shasta Daisy, and Marguerite.

Sunflower or Daisy family
Up to 3 ft tall
Flowers in May-August
Also grows in fields and yards

Common Mouse-ear Chickweed

Mouse-ear Chickweeds get their name from their gray-green leaves, which are covered with short downy hairs and look like furry mice's ears. Each flower has five hairy sepals and five, deeply-notched, white petals. The flowers grow in clusters at the end of the flower stems. The rest of the plant creeps along the ground, putting down roots from time to time.

Pink family
Up to 12 ins tall
Flowers in June-September
Also grows in lawns and fields

Pearly Everlasting

This plant is called everlasting because its dry, papery flowers last much longer than most flowers, and are often used as dried flowers. The flower heads grow in branched clusters at the tops of the stems. Look for the white, papery bracts around the yellow centers. It is these bracts which last so long. Look at the stem and narrow leaves, too—they are covered in white, woolly hairs.

Sunflower or Daisy family
2–3 ft tall
Flowers in July-September
Also grows in yards and dry open places but not in the southern US

Yarrow

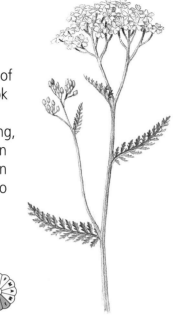

Look for the fairly flat clusters of small, white flower heads. Look for its soft, ferny, dark green leaves, too. Yarrow has creeping, underground roots which often nurture large colonies. It has an aromatic smell and was used to stop bleeding. It was used to dress wounds for more than three thousand years.

Sunflower or Daisy family
1–3 ft tall
Flowers in June-September
Also grows in fields

Queen Anne's Lace

You will easily see these large, flat umbels of creamy-white flowers. Look for the one purple or red flower in the center of each umbel. The leaves are fern-like, and alternate up the stem. When the flowers die, the umbels close up and look like birds' nests with many spiky fruits. Also known as Wild Carrot, it has swollen fleshy roots like cultivated carrots, but smaller, with a carroty smell.

Carrot or Parsley family
1–3 ft tall
Flowers in May-October
Also grows in fields and meadows

Wild Mint

You can easily find this flower because of its strong smell. It often grows in fields of peppermint, but has to be weeded out because it ruins the flavor. The flowers are white, pale pink, or lavender, and grow in thick whorls from the bases of the leaf stalks of the upper leaves. The opposite leaves are oval and toothed. Look at the stems—some creep along the ground, others grow straight up.

Mint family
Up to 2 ft tall
Flowers in May-August
Also grows along streams and in wet meadows

Bull Thistle

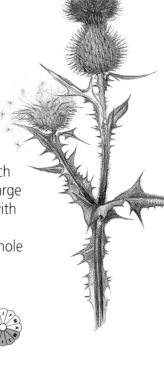

Thistles have spiny stems and spiny leaves. Even the swollen base of the flower is covered with prickly bracts. The red-purple flower of the Bull Thistle is followed by a ball of fluffy, white seeds which blow away in the wind. The large leaves are lobed and tipped with spines. Look out for the spiny wings which run down the whole length of the stem as well.

Sunflower or Daisy family
Up to 6 ft tall
Flowers in May-August
Also grows in fields, pastures and meadows

New England Aster

You may see this flower growing in yards or in tall clumps alongside streams. The purplish red flowers have yellow centers and grow on flower heads among the upper leaves. Feel how sticky the long flower stalks are. The leaves are lance-shaped, and alternate up the hairy stems.

Sunflower or Daisy family
Up to 7 ft tall
Flowers in July-October
Also grows in wet meadows and swamps, mainly in the central US

Selfheal

As the name says, this plant was once used to help wounds and sore throats to heal. It is hardly ever used as a medicine today, however. The blue-violet flowers grow in thick clusters at the tops of the stems. Look for their two lips and their hairy bracts. The leaves are egg- or lance-shaped, and are unequally toothed. They grow in opposite pairs on short stalks.

Mint family
6–12 ins tall
Flowers in May-September
Also grows in fields and lawns

Common Mallow

The Common Mallow has sprawling, branched stems covered with lots of downy hairs. The flowers are white, veined, and tinged with pink or purple. They grow in clusters from the base of the long leaf stems. Look for the palmate leaves and for the fruits. Mallows are often called Cheeses because each fruit looks like a round cheese cut into pieces.

Mallow family
Up to 2 ft tall
Flowers in April-October
Also grows in yards

White Clover

You can easily recognize White Clover from its leaves, which are divided into three rounded leaflets. Look for the white band around the base of each leaflet. The thick, white or pink flower heads grow from the base of the leafstalk. All clovers are rich in nectar. Look for bees probing into the many small flowers that make up the flower head. Some of the best honey is made from clover.

Pea and Bean family
Up to 1 ft tall – Flowers in May-September
Also grows on lawns

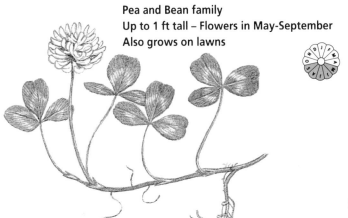

Jimsonweed

Be very careful of Jimsonweed. All parts of the plant are very poisonous. The seeds grow in prickly, egg-shaped capsules. The whole plant looks very coarse, and gives off a strong odor. The white or violet petals of the flower form a long trumpet, the lower part of which is enclosed by the sepals. The leaves are large, egg-shaped, and lobed. The stem is coarse and purplish with many branches.

Nightshade family
Up to 5 ft tall – Flowers in May-September
Also grows on pastures

Field Bindweed

Bindweed is easy to recognize. It is a creeping or climbing vine with pink or white flowers and arrowhead-shaped leaves. See how the five petals of each flower join together to make a funnel. Look for Field Bindweed straggling over the ground. You won't see the roots, but they go deep underground, up to 6 feet or more.

Morning Glory family
Creeping vine 3–10 ft long
Flowers in May-August

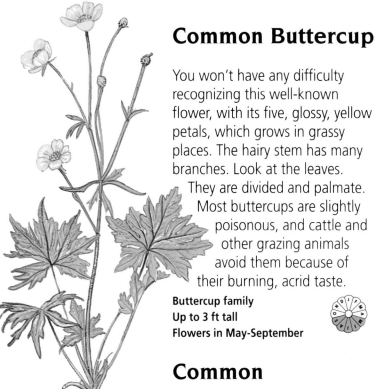

Common Buttercup

You won't have any difficulty recognizing this well-known flower, with its five, glossy, yellow petals, which grows in grassy places. The hairy stem has many branches. Look at the leaves. They are divided and palmate. Most buttercups are slightly poisonous, and cattle and other grazing animals avoid them because of their burning, acrid taste.

Buttercup family
Up to 3 ft tall
Flowers in May-September

Common Evening Primrose

These showy, yellow flowers open a few at a time and only in the evening. They close by noon the next day. Each flower has four petals and eight prominent stamens. Alternating, lance-shaped leaves with wavy, slightly-toothed edges grow thickly on an erect, unbranched stem. The flowers are followed by large, oblong capsules which stand up, more or less.

Evening Primrose family
Up to 5 ft tall
Flowers in May-August

Woolly Sunflower

You will easily recognize this plant with its many, solitary, yellow flowers, and gray leaves and stems. They look gray because they are covered with gray-white, woolly hairs, which give the plant its name. The hairs help the plant retain water, and so to grow in dry, sunny places. The lower leaves are narrow and divided. The upper leaves are narrow, but not divided.

Sunflower or Daisy family
12–30 ins tall
Flowers in May-August
Also grows in yards and dry places in western states

Sticky Cinquefoil

This plant grows in open places in western states. The flowers of Sticky Cinquefoil vary from pale yellow to creamy-white. They grow in loose clusters at the end of reddish flowering stems which grow upward. The stems grow in clumps and have special glands which make them sticky. The lower leaves are pinnate with five to nine, toothed, egg-shaped leaflets.

Rose family
Up to 2ft tall
Flowers in May-July

Cowpen Daisy

These flowers are bright yellow and grow in broad flower heads at the end of long flower stalks. Look for the toothed, outer ray flowers growing around the yellow center. The toothed triangular leaves are gray-green. The stems have many branches and, if you look closely, you can see they are covered with tiny hairs. It is also called Golden Crownbeard.

Sunflower or Daisy family
1–5 ft tall
Flowers in June-September
Also grows on ranges and pastures in western states

Common St John's-wort

These little yellow flowers have five pointed petals and many stamens. Look closely at the petals and you can see they have tiny, black dots around the edges. The leaves are narrow, canoe-shaped, and grow in pairs. If you hold one of the leaves up to the light you can see that it is covered by translucent dots.

St John's-wort family
15–30 ins tall
Flowers in May-August
Also grows in meadows

Black Mustard

You will easily spot these bright yellow flowers, which add a splash of color to roadsides and fields. The lower leaves are large, bristley, and lobed. The upper leaves are smaller and toothed. The flowers are followed by long pods which press against the stem. In Europe, Black Mustard is farmed for its seeds, but in North America it is regarded as a weed. It is closely related to broccoli, cabbage, cauliflower, and Brussels sprouts.

Mustard family
Up to 3 ft tall
Flowers in June-October
Also grows in fields

Dandelion

Dandelions are one of the best-known flowers, but look for its rosette of wavy, lobed, and toothed leaves. The stalks are hollow, and they and the leaves ooze a milky juice if broken. The flower heads are followed by balls of parachuted seeds which are scattered in the wind. The leaves can be eaten in salads, and the roots can be roasted and ground to make a coffee substitute.

Sunflower or Daisy family
2–18 ins tall
Flowers in March-September
Also grows on lawns and other grassy places, in fields and pastures

Bird's-foot Trefoil

Look for this bright yellow flower among the plants where it grows in grassy places and on the sides of roads. The flowers grow on long stalks from the base of a leaf. The leaves are divided into three small leaflets. The flowers yield to long pods which look like a bird's foot, but they are hard to find before they twist and split open to release the seeds.

Pea and Bean family
Up to 2 ft tall
Flowers in May-August
Also grows in fields

Yellow Salsify

These showy, pale yellow flowers are easy to find. Look for the long, slender, green bracts which protect the flowers when they are closed and extend beyond the ray flowers when they are open. Look at the stems, too. They swell just below the flower heads. If you break a stem, milky juice oozes out. The flower heads are followed by large, spectacular balls of feathery parachutes, each one attached to a seed.

Sunflower or Daisy family
12–30 ins tall
Flowers in May-September
Also grows on dry, open places

Butter-and-eggs

You will be able to see this bright cluster of yellow and orange flowers easily. The plant forms large colonies of leafy stems which grow upward, and yellow spikes of flowers. Look carefully at the flowers. Each has two lips with a straight spur at the bottom of the flower and orange inside. In herbal medicine the plant was used to treat jaundice. If it is soaked in milk, it also makes a good fly killer.

Snapdragon or Figwort family
1–3 ft tall
Flowers in May-October
Also grows along railroads and in dry fields

Canadian Goldenrod

You can't miss the long, glowing yellow plumes of Goldenrod. It grows in woodland clearings and open places except in the southern US. The flowers are made up of masses of tiny flowers which grow on many short, arching branches at the top of the stem. The tall stems, which grow upward, sway in the wind and are covered with many lance-shaped leaves which alternate up them.

Sunflower or Daisy family
Up to 5 ft tall
Flowers in May-November

Tansy

These yellow flower heads are easy to recognize. They are composed of tiny disk flowers and few or no ray flowers. These grow in flat-topped clusters on branches of small stalks. The stems are straight and strong and the alternate leaves are soft and divided into fern-like, toothed segments. Tansy was used to bathe sprains and bruises. It also repels insects which don't like its bitter smell.

Sunflower or Daisy family
2–3 ft tall
Flowers in July-September
Also grows in fields

Common Mullein

This tall, sturdy plant has long, yellow spikes of flowers and unusual leaves. It grows well in dry places because the leaves channel rainwater down the stem into the roots. The leaves are also covered with woolly down which stops them from drying out. People have used the leaves for rouge, as shoe liners, in tobacco, and as a remedy for chest diseases.

Snapdragon or Figwort family
Up to 6 ft tall
Flowers in May-August
Also grows in fields

Black-eyed Susan

You won't miss these showy yellow flowers. Each flower head is 2–3 inches across and has a brown center, surrounded by up to 20 golden-yellow ray flowers. Feel the leaves. They are rough with coarse hairs. They vary in shape and may be lance-shaped, oval or egg-shaped, with or without teeth.

Sunflower or Daisy family
1–3 ft tall – Flowers in June-October
Also grows on hillsides, prairies, fields, and open woods in southern Canada and most of the US

Day Lily

These tawny-orange flowers are shaped like a funnel, and grow in clusters at the end of long, bare stems. The bright green leaves are shaped like broad blades of grass, and grow together in clumps at the base of the plant. Day Lilies are well-known yard plants, but many have escaped to grow wild on roadsides and in meadows. They were originally brought to North America from Japan.

Lily family
Up to 4 ft tall – Flowers in May-July
Also grows in yards

Butterfly-weed

This plant gets its name because its orange flowers attracts many butterflies. Each flower has five back-curving petals and a five-part central crown. Look for them in large umbels near the top of the leafy stems which grow upward. They are followed by large pods of hairy seeds. This plant is also called Pleurisy Root and was used in Native American and herbal medicine to treat pleurisy, bronchitis, pneumonia, whooping cough, and other chest diseases.

Milkweed family
Up to 30 ins tall
Flowers in May-August
Also grows in dry open fields, meadows, and prairies in the eastern, midwestern and southern US

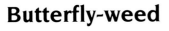

Red Clover

To tell Red Clover apart from White Clover with a pink flower (see page 67), look at the leaves. Red Clover has a light V-shaped pattern on the leaflets. The pink-purple flower clusters grow between two leaves at the ends of the stems. Clover petals stay on the flower head after they have withered. Look then for the seed pods in the brown flower heads.

Pea and Bean family
Up to 2 ft tall
Flowers in May-September
Also grows in fields

Red Maids

You will easily see these small, but brilliant, bright rose-red flowers. The plant has several spreading stems and narrow leaves. The leaves are fleshy, telling you that this plant is a succulent. You will find it growing in grassy places in the western US where there is water early in the year.

Purslane family
4–16 ins tall
Flowers in March-April

Pasture Rose

It is easy to see this flower is a rose. It has five, heart-shaped, pink petals and lots of stamens in the center. The arching stems are protected by stiff hairs and straight thorns. The compound leaves are divided into three to seven oval leaflets. The flowers are followed by bright red fruits called hips. Rose hip syrup, jelly, and tea are made from them, and they are rich in Vitamin C and minerals.

Rose family
Up to 3 ft tall – Flowers in April-June
Also grows in grasslands and
dry woods in eastern states

Scarlet Pimpernel

You will only see these attractive red or orange flowers fully open on bright, sunny mornings. They close at about 3.00 pm, and stay closed in cloudy weather. Look for the sprawling stems and pointed, egg-shaped leaves which grow in opposite pairs. Look for the seed capsules, too. They have hinged lids which open to release the seeds.

Primrose family
Low-growing, 4–12 ins tall
Flowers in June-August
Also grows in sandy places

Lady's Thumb

You will find this plant almost everywhere on damp, cultivated land and desolate ground. Its many pink flowers grow in thick spikes at the end of the stems which grow upward. Look at the leaves, too. They are small and lance-shaped with a dark green triangle on each one.

Buckwheat family
8–32 ins tall
Flowers in
June-September

Spotted Knapweed

At first glance knapweeds look a lot like thistles, but they don't have spines or prickles. You can tell Spotted Knapweed apart from the other knapweeds by looking at the swollen base under the pink-purple flower head. It is spotted with black-tipped bracts. The stem is branched and wiry, and the long, narrow leaves are divided into segments.

Sunflower or Daisy family
Up to 3 ft tall
Flowers in June-August
Also grows in fields and pastures in eastern states

Smooth Aster

Look for the Smooth Aster's purple flowers with yellow centers. The stems and leaves are smooth and often look grayish. The narrow leaves alternate up the stems. See how the base of the leaves seem to grip the stem.

Sunflower or Daisy family
Up to 4 ft tall
Flowers in April-July
Also grows in dry, open places in eastern Canada and US

Teasel

Teasels grow in wet places. They have upright, prickly stems and prickly leaves. The lower leaves join across the stem making a cup to collect water and drown insects who might attack the plant. The tiny pale purple flowers grow together in a cone-shaped head. The flowers in the center open first and new ones open daily toward the top and bottom, forming two bands that move in opposite directions. Look for the dead, dried flower heads right through the winter.

Teasel family – Up to 6 ft tall
Flowers in July-October

Common Morning Glory

Morning Glory is really a tropical plant. It was brought here from tropical America as a yard plant. The funnel-shaped flowers can be blue, purple, pink, or white. They grow from the base of the leaves which are broad and heart-shaped. The stems form a twining vine, and if you look closely you can see they are covered in hairs.

Morning Glory family
Creeping vine up to 10 ft long
Flowers in July-October
Also grows in fields, thickets, and yards in the eastern states

Common Burdock

The pink or lavender flowers peep out of the top of the swollen base. Look for the hooked bracts which cover the base. The flowers are followed by hooked burs which cling to animals' fur, and maybe even to your own clothes. Look at the leaves, too. They have long, hollow stalks and are egg-shaped or heart-shaped, particularly lower down the stem. The reddish stems form a bushy plant with many branches.

Sunflower or Daisy family
About 5 ft tall
Flowers in May-August
Also grows in old fields

Common Milkweed

Look at the top of the stem for the drooping umbels of the dull purplish flowers which grow from the base of the leaf stems. Each flower has five back-curved petals and a five-part crown which grows upward. They are followed by large, upright pods of seeds attached to hairy parachutes. The leaves are opposite, oblong, and covered with downy hairs underneath. The stems of milkweeds contain a poisonous milky juice.

Milkweed family
Up to 6 ft tall – Flowers in June-August
Also grows in old fields in the eastern and midwestern US

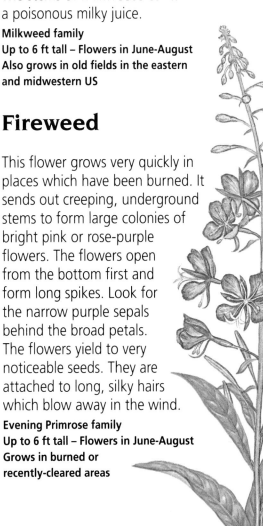

Crown Vetch

This small, straggling plant was brought to North America as a yard plant, but has escaped into the wild and grows in grassy places. Look for the round clusters of pink flowers on long flower stalks which grow from the base of the leaves. The compound leaves have only 15 to 20 leaflets each. Look for the upright seed pods which follow the flowers.

Pea and Bean family
1–2 ft tall
Flowers in May-August

Fireweed

This flower grows very quickly in places which have been burned. It sends out creeping, underground stems to form large colonies of bright pink or rose-purple flowers. The flowers open from the bottom first and form long spikes. Look for the narrow purple sepals behind the broad petals. The flowers yield to very noticeable seeds. They are attached to long, silky hairs which blow away in the wind.

Evening Primrose family
Up to 6 ft tall – Flowers in June-August
Grows in burned or recently-cleared areas

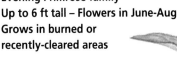

Bachelor's Buttons

These deep blue flower heads are hard to miss. The leaves are narrow and the stem is slender and wiry and grows upward. Look carefully at the flower heads. The blue disk flowers are tubular. Underneath the flower head is the hard, round seedbox, covered with fringed bracts. This flower, when grown in yards, can sometimes be pink or white.

Sunflower or Daisy family
Up to 3 ft tall
Flowers in May-August
Also grows in fields
and yards

Lesser Periwinkle

The Lesser Periwinkle does not grow very high, so you might have to look carefully for its small, bright blue flowers among the other plants. The five petals all curve the same way so the flower looks like a wheel with a white hub at the center. The leaves are dark green, and grow opposite each other. Periwinkles were originally brought from Europe as yard flowers.

Dogbane family
Up to 7 ins high
Flowers in April-May
Also grows in yards
and borders of woods

Harebell

This nodding, bell-shaped flower is easy to see because it grows on such sparse land. You may see it all the way across Canada, in northern US states and in the western mountains. Look for the narrow leaves and five joined petals. This delicate flower has many other names—Bluebell, Fairy Bells, Lady's Thimbles, and Sheep Bells—because it often grows where sheep like to graze.

Bellflower or Bluebell family
Up to 20 ins tall
Flowers in June-September
Also grows on dry grassland,
cliffs, and rocky areas

Bluet

These little, sky-blue flowers have yellow centers and grow at the end of thin, straight stalks. The small, oval leaves grow up the stalk in opposite pairs. Look for the larger leaves at the base of the stems.

Bedstraw or Madder family
3–6 ins tall
Flowers in April-June
Grows in lawns, meadows and
fields in eastern states

Asiatic Dayflower

Once you have found this sprawling plant it is easy to recognize it because of its flowers. Each small flower has two large blue petals and one smaller whitish one. The leaves are lance-shaped and alternate up the stem.

Spiderwort family
1–3 ft tall – Flowers in June-October
Also grows in borders of woodlands
in eastern states

Chicory

The bright blue flowers of Chicory are easy to see, even from a moving car. If you can, look for the rosette of wavy, toothed leaves at the base of the stalk. The young shoots can be eaten raw in salads or cooked as a vegetable. In Europe, its roots are roasted and ground, and added to coffee or drunk instead of coffee.

Sunflower or Daisy family
Up to 4 ft tall
Flowers in May-August
Also grows in fields

Virginia Spiderwort

You may not see the Virginia Spiderwort's blue or purple flowers immediately. They can be hidden by the bracts, which are longer and wider than the leaves. The plant grows in clumps of tall stems which grow upward, but they are hidden by the long, interlocking leaves, as well.

Spiderwort family
Up to 2 ft tall
Flowers in April-July
Also grows in damp woodlands and meadows, mainly in the South

Find Out Some More

Useful Organizations

In addition to the national groups listed below, there are hundreds of local natural history associations. Check with your nearest natural history museum, your school, or local public library for information on them.

The **National Wildflower Research Center** is one of the best beginning points for wild flower buffs; their *Wildflower Handbook* provides information on organizations, gardens and resources in all 50 states. Write to: National Wildflower Research Center, 2600 FM 973 North, Austin, Texas 78725; (512) 929–3600.

In Canada, the **Canadian Wildflower Society** is your best starting point. Write to the Canadian Wildflower Society, 35 Bauer Crescent, Unionville, Ontario, L3R 4H3.

Or you could try the **Canadian Botanical Association**. Write to: Canadian Botanical Association, Dept. of Botany. University of British Columbia, Vancouver, British Columbia V6T 2BI.

Many of the preserves owned by the **Nature Conservancy** and its chapters, conserve unique and threatened wildflower habitats. Write to: Nature Conservancy, Suite 800, 1800 N. Kent Street, Arlington, VA 22209.

The **American Association of Botanical Gardens and Arboreta** is the best source of information about botanical gardens. Across the country, they are increasingly featuring native wild flowers. While not wild habitats, they provide a good chance to see otherwise rare species and some are devoted exclusively to wild flowers. Write to: American Association of Botanical Gardens and Arboreta, University of Alberta, Edmonton, Alberta, T5K 2C9.

Places To Visit

Wild flowers can be as easy to find as stopping along a country road, but the following locations are especially good for variety.

In the **East**, Bartholomew's Cobble, Massachusetts boasts one of the most all-inclusive wild flower communities in the country, while in Pennsylvania, the Shenk's Ferry Glen Wildflower Preserve and Enlow Fork Natural Area are superb. Bog plants, including orchids, bloom in midsummer at Cranberry Glades Botanical Area, Monongahela National Forest in West Virginia. For eastern forests, try visiting the Adirondack Forest Preserve in New York, the Great Smoky Mountains National Park in Tennesee, or the Shenandoah National Park in Virginia.

In the **Plains**, remnant prairies still burst in flower in summer at Konza Prairie and Flint Hills Tallgrass Prairie, Kansas; at Pawnee Prairie and Valentine National Wildlife Refuge in Nebraska; at the Curlew Prairie in Iowa; and at Hoosier Prairie Nature Reserve in Indiana.

In the **Southwest and California deserts**, a wet winter may produce astonishing blooms from the normally arid land; February, March and April are best in southern Arizona and New Mexico. Try Organ Pipe Cactus National Monument in Arizona to see cacti.

In the **West**, perhaps no wildflower spectacle matches the bloom of California's wild poppies, especially at the Californian State Antelope Valley Poppy Reserve, where the land turns orange to the horizon. For western forests, visit Rocky Mountain National Park in Colorado, Yellowstone National Park in Wyoming, or Crater Lake National Park in Oregon.

Index & Glossary

To find the name of a plant in this index, search under its main name. So, to look up Yellow-eyed Grass; look under Grass, not under Yellow-eyed.

Useful Books

As well as the general books listed here, there are many that deal with the wild flowers of specific states, provinces, and regions; ask your local reference librarian to recommend some for your area.

Wild Plants of America, Richard M. Smith (John Wiley & Sons, 1989) An excellent guide to the best natural places in the United States to find a variety of wild flowers.

Wildflowers, Rick Imes (Rodale Press, 1992) An identification guide with information on growing wild flowers in the home garden.

How to Know the Wildflowers, Mrs. William Starr Dana (Houghton Mifflin Co., 1981 reissue) Chatty folklore book—a reissue of an 1893 classic.

Newcomb's Wildflower Guide, Lawrence Newcomb (Little Brown, 1977) Unique key approach to northeastern wild flowers.

Weeds in Winter, Lauren Brown (W.W. Norton, 1976) Illustrates 135 common plants, mostly wild flowers

Index & Glossary